SLS 1510
Your Passport to Success

Second Edition
Revised Printing

SLS Department
Tallahassee Community College

Kendall Hunt
publishing company
4050 Westmark Drive • P O Box 1840 • Dubuque IA 52004-1840

To Our Students Past, Present and Future

Executive Editor: *Gayle Fisher, Department Head College Success*
Managing Editor: *Lynn Burgess*

Project Editors: *Rick Groshong*
Craig Fletcher

Cover Design: *Rob Chaney*
Skip Greenfield
Rhoddy McKown

The editors would also like to acknowledge the contributions and input of the faculty, staff, and students whose input has been invaluable to this project.

Special thanks to Dr. Sally Search, our Dean, for giving us the freedom to create and for supporting us in this effort to produce our best work so that our students will benefit.

ACKNOWLEDGEMENTS

We continue to gratefully acknowledge the contributions of the following authors who contributed their writing skills, proofreading skills, and time to make the first edition of this textbook possible: Mike Culligan, Doug Davey, Robin Donaldson, Gayle Fisher, Rebecca Gubitti, Robin Haggins, Leslie Harper, Kim Manning, Patrick McDermott, Deborah Schaum, Jennifer Siegel, Sally Search, and Rebecca Vick.

And to our first editor and the cover designers who gave our collective work one voice:
Margie Menzel, Mark Lowe, and Rhoddy McKown.

Contents

Introduction to TCC and College Success

Welcome to SLS1510: College Success. And, welcome to Tallahassee Community College. This class and this textbook are intended to help you improve your level of success this semester, throughout the rest of your college career, and in your life.

One of the most fundamental ways to understand the word "success" is to think of it as "achieving what you try to achieve." This brings up two key ideas. First, success requires effort. If you don't *try*, you cannot achieve what you are trying to achieve. Second, what counts as success will vary from one person to the next. If you achieve what *you* try to achieve, you have succeeded (on your terms).

One of the recurring themes of this book will be to think carefully about what you are doing and why. In order to improve your habits, you need to understand what you are doing and why you are doing it. The more carefully you think about the topics we address, the more you will benefit from this class.

ENSURING SUCCESS

Success has three basic requirements: you must know where you want to go, how you will get there, and from where you are starting. Therefore, in this class we will have three basic tasks.

First, we will conduct a number of self-assessment surveys. If you understand more clearly what skills you have or don't have, you can target your efforts more effectively. For example, there are several different "learning styles"—understanding how you learn best will help you study better.

Second, we will explore how to set goals and figure out what you want to achieve. We will discuss careers and majors as well as personal goals.

Third, we will spend time developing the skills one needs to reach goals. We will look at how to budget time and money, how to study and take notes, and how to develop good habits in many other areas of life.

Much of the content of this class is about forming good habits, not learning specific information. Take the exercises and activities seriously and they will help you not only in this class, but throughout your college career.

EXPECTATIONS

Students in two freshmen level courses were asked to describe the transitional issues they faced in their first semester and we will build upon their experiences to explain this concept of **transition**.

Personal Responsibility

"In college you have freedom to do as you please . . . to go where you wish . . . to do as you wish. Unfortunately, this freedom is easily abused. The student carries 98% of the responsibility and control."

Those of you entering college from high school know that freedom is a new experience for you, especially where school is concerned. For the first time in your school career no one is going to remind you of assignments, tests, or your attendance. For those of you who are returning to school, you may be used to freedom, but your challenge will be to not allow your freedom to impede your success in school. If you are working and attending school, freedom may become a burden that allows you to put off until the last minute the things you need to do for school thus creating an environment of stress and confusion that you have not before been acquainted with.

Class Attendance

"As a college student, you will decide whether you want to go to class or not. Being absent will hurt you in the long run."

No matter where you are transitioning from, the concept of attending class is a big one. In SLS we take roll each day, expect you to be in class, and expect you to participate. While some classes may not be this way, don't fall into the trap of not attending class. One of the best and easiest ways to do well in class is to be there every day. Remember, if you don't hear the instructor say something in class, when it appears on a test, you will have no idea how to answer. BE RESPONSIBLE. Don't miss class.

Teacher Attitudes

"Your instructors will not hound you to do your work. It's entirely up to you." "Get to know your teachers. If your teachers know you, it will be easier for them to look out for you and help you if you're having trouble."

Our student teacher ratio in SLS is 28–30:1, but this may not be the case in all classes. If you don't know your teacher's name or where their office is located, then you are not making an effort to be a part of the class. Teachers respond more quickly to students who participate, do their work, and who attend class. No matter where you are transitioning from learn this lesson. Use the quick look in the front of your textbook so you can reference back to the teacher's name.

Types of Assignments

"In high school we were given a homework assignment every day. Now we have a large task assigned to be done at a certain time. No one tells you when to start or what to do each day. Once you get an assignment, start working on it right away. It takes a daily effort to keep up."

No two classes will have the same types of assignments. That is why in this class we attempt to introduce you to a variety of assignment types so that you can learn the differences. Whatever the assignment, learn to *write down due dates*, put reminders in your planner, and devise some type of checklist to ensure you have completed all parts of the assignment. Most instructors will provide a guide sheet for the assignment. DON'T lose it. USE it!

Time Management

"The amount of free time you have in college is much more than in high school. Always have a weekly study schedule to go by. Otherwise, time slips away and you will not be able to account for it."

In this class we devote an entire chapter to time management. It truly is the key to your success in college and, ultimately, in life. If you currently use a planner to manage your time, you are on the right track; however, if you don't, this is the time to start. There are any number of things we can say about time management, but the most effective way to teach you the concept, no matter what background you come from, is to use the time management exercise in Chapter 6. Once you have figured out the total number of hours you have free each week, we will transfer this topic over to the chapter on time management and discuss it in detail.

Difficulty of College Work

"College is probably going to be tougher than high school. Don't let that stop you!"

There's no doubt about it. The level of work and the amount of work required in college is more than you ever experienced in high school. If you have been out of high school for a while and are returning, this may be one of the biggest hindrances you face. Start slowly. Since 12 hours is considered full-time, don't overload your first couple of semesters. To put it in practical terms, 12 hours of classes is equivalent to having a full-time job. Take classes seriously and listen to your advisor. They really do know what they're talking about. If you become overwhelmed and think you need to drop a class, talk to your teacher first, then your advisor. They may be able to help you develop a plan to get you through. Also, if you do have to drop a class, learn from that and don't make the same mistake the next semester.

Social Life

"Sometimes it seems harder to make friends because of the size of the school. But there are a variety of organizations and activities. Get involved and meet the people!"

While the primary reason you are attending TCC is to get an education, don't ignore the need to socialize. But be smart about how you choose to do it. Use TCC resources as a starting point. Get involved in your campus and begin to make friends here. Don't, however, let anyone influence you to do something you don't want to do. And, always remember that social activities should come only **after** you have fulfilled the obligations that are part of your daily schedule. Plan time for fun, but plan it wisely.

ASSESSMENTS

As part of the self-assessment portion of this class, you will be asked to respond to a number of different surveys. Your instructor will assign a personality-type assessment, which you will either do online or in the Career Center on campus. Your instructor will also ask you to complete the Self-Directed Search (SDS) career interest booklet. There are a number of worksheets and exercises in this textbook as well.

SUMMARY

So, are you ready to begin? Welcome to College Success, to TCC and to the life of a college student. Let's get started.

You can choose to be successful, or you can let chance rule your life. The decision is yours.

SUCCESS: CHANCE OR CHOICE?

CHOOSING SUCCESS	LETTING CHANCE RULE
You have the mindset for success. Your attitude is positive, hopeful, and future-oriented.	You have the mindset for failure. Your attitude is negative, self-sabotaging, and past-oriented.
You take personal responsibility for whatever happens in your life. You believe you hold the power.	You see yourself as a victim of circumstance, luck, fate, or people in power.
You are self-motivated. You see the connection between actions and outcomes.	You lack motivation. You see no connection between actions and outcomes.
You are self-determining. You set goals, make plans, and stay on course.	You lack direction. You act on impulse rather than planning. You procrastinate and lose sight of your goals.
You are self-regulating. You control your emotions, interact well with others, and know when to ask for help.	You let your emotions control you. Your interpersonal skills are lacking, and you often reject offers of help.
You are flexible. You adapt well to change and will try new strategies.	You are rigid. You adapt poorly to change and resist trying new strategies.
For you, college is an experience and you are fully involved. You believe in lifelong learning.	For you, college is something to get out of the way so you can get on with your life. You believe in learning only enough to get by.
You are persistent. For you, mistakes are instructive and failure is a temporary setback that you can overcome.	You give up too easily and do not learn from mistakes. For you, failure seems like a permanent condition over which you are powerless.
The bottom line is that you believe in yourself and will do what it takes to succeed.	The bottom line is that you lack faith in yourself and consistently avoid taking steps that would lead to success.

Chapter 1

Knowing My Campus

LEARNING OBJECTIVES

By the end of this chapter you should be able to:

Discuss TCC's resources for students

Know where to find help, and how to get it

Know how to become involved with campus activities at TCC

ABOUT TALLAHASSEE COMMUNITY COLLEGE (TCC)

Approximately 75% of TCC's 14,000 students plan to earn degrees in the Associate of Arts transfer program. TCC is Florida State University's largest feeder institution and has an excellent relationship with FSU, Florida A&M University, and other centers of learning. The College offers an Associate in Science degree in 15 fields, including business administration, computer programming, digital broadcasting, graphic design, criminal justice technology, and paralegal and legal studies. TCC also offers courses for credit at off-campus sites, including its centers in Quincy and Crawfordville, and via television, the Internet, and independent study. To satisfy community needs and promote lifelong learning, TCC offers noncredit programs, professional development seminars, and personal enrichment classes.

HERE ARE SOME KEY RESOURCES TO HELP YOU BE A SUCCESSFUL STUDENT:

Faculty

Your instructors are your most important resource during your college career. Faculty members are selected based on proven teaching ability. In fact, teaching is their main job. Unlike university professors who are also expected to publish scholarly works, the members of TCC's faculty devote nearly all of their time to classroom instruction, advising students one-on-one, and helping them adapt to college. Office hours and email make your instructors highly accessible to you; however, you must take the initiative. Early in the semester make sure you introduce yourself to each of your instructors and locate their offices.

Student Access Card

Your key to TCC services is your *Student Access Card*, or ID. Cards are issued in the Student Union, Room 273, from 8:00 a.m. to 7:00 p.m., Monday through Thursday, and from 8:00 a.m. to 5:00 p.m. on Friday. Photo identification (i.e., a driver's license) is required. An Access Card has uses both on and off campus, so you'll want to get yours within the first two weeks of class. Among other things, on campus the card allows you to check out library materials, conduct online research, use the Lifetime Sports Complex, and use the student computer labs. Off campus it allows you to ride Tallahassee Star Metro busses for free, provides free or reduced access to county parks and recreation (including swimming pools), discounts at many area businesses, and more.

Academic Computing Labs

    AC210: (850) 201-8268

    CT206: (850) 201-8627

The academic computing labs are available to TCC students, faculty, and staff with validated TCC Access Cards. Labs are located in Academic Computing 210 and 211, Technology and Professional Programs 211, and Computer Technology 206. Students are welcome to use the labs' hardware and software to complete their course assignments. Available software includes Microsoft Word, Excel, PowerPoint, Access, and multimedia applications. Macintosh platforms can be found in the AC201, AC211, and CT206 labs. And, of course, students can access the Internet and use other computer-related equipment such as CD-ROMs and scanners.

The Student Technology Assistance Resource (STAR) lab, in the Learning Commons, boosts students' computer skills with online tutorials and one-on-one assistance. So that students can practice their PowerPoint presentations, the STAR Lab is equipped with a computer projector, as well as ample space to meet and work on group projects.

There is an additional computer lab located in the library. See below for additional information.

TCC Learning Commons

The TCC Learning Commons is a comprehensive, integrated learning center that provides learning assistance and resources to all TCC students. The Learning Commons offers students and faculty a broad range of services including diagnostic assessments, learning materials and electronic resources, individual conferences, one-on-one and small group tutoring, whole class support, workshops and seminars, success strategies, technology and multi-media support, and assistance developing and assessing Individual Learning plans. Throughout the Learning Commons, students have open access to computers, computer applications, and technology support.

The first floor of the Learning Commons provides support for students in all levels of mathematics, business related courses, health sciences, physical sciences, and natural sciences. The second floor provides support for students in all aspects of communication including reading, writing, language skills, and support for nonnative speakers of English. Services in the Learning Commons are provided using a differentiated staffing approach where the needs of the student are matched with various specialized skills of staff members.

- Learning specialists and faculty collaborate to assist students in identifying and using resources to maximize learning and support student success.
- Student success specialists from the Student Success Center provide advising, study skills seminars, and counseling support.
- Communication specialists and library staff collaborate to provide support for research and information literacy.

The goal of the Learning Commons is to be *proactive* in helping students identify their learning needs and then use the resources and services that are available to improve their academic performance.

Learning Services

Learning services include self-help, brief staff-assisted, and intensive staff-assisted services that are delivered by staff members to assist students in improving their academic performance.

Self-help services involve self-guided use of self-assessments and information resources in resource areas or on websites, where resources have been designed for independent use by students with a *high* readiness for learning.

Brief staff-assisted services involve staff member or faculty-guided use of assessment, information, and instructional materials and multimedia in resource areas, classrooms, or group settings for students with *moderate* readiness for learning.

- *Drop-in services* involve practitioner-guided use of learning resources for students in the Learning Commons, with support provided by practitioners on an as-needed basis.
- *Academic support courses* involve faculty-guided use of learning resources in a classroom setting, as well as staff-guided use of learning resources in the Learning Commons.

- *Peer learning groups* involve students working collaboratively to learn and apply specific academic skills, with staff support provided as needed.
- *Workshops* involve presentations by staff members on topics related to improving student academic performance and may include guided use of learning resources in groups.

Intensive Staff-Assisted Services involve faculty or staff member-guided use of assessment, information, and instructional materials and multimedia in an individual office or group setting for students needing intensive guidance to ensure learning. These students include those in the following situations:

- *Academic support courses* involve faculty-guided use of learning resources in a classroom setting, as well as staff-guided use of learning resources in the Learning Commons. Students will have an individual learning plan developed by their instructor, plus individualized assistance from their instructor and staff members.
- *Individual tutoring* will be offered for drop-in students who are referred to the Learning Commons by their instructors.

Library

(850) 201-8396 (circulation)

(850) 201-8383 (reference)

Hours of operation:

Monday through Thursday: 7:30 a.m. to 9:00 p.m.

Friday: 7:30 a.m. to 5:00 p.m.

Saturday: 10:00 a.m. to 2:00 p.m.

The TCC Library houses a substantial collection of materials appropriate to the College's curriculum and to student interests. The collection includes books, periodicals, pamphlets, microfilm, videotapes, DVDs, CDs, computer software, and extensive online resources. For students with disabilities, materials and equipment—including adaptive technology—are available. Professional librarians and skilled support staff provide services to help students prepare their assignments and pursue other educational and personal interests. While the book, magazine, and newspaper areas are open to anyone visiting the library, circulating materials can be checked out for 2 weeks at a time by students, faculty, and staff. Instructional handouts and individual assistance are available whenever the library is open.

To check out materials or to use the library's computer lab, study rooms, or reserve audio-visual materials, a valid TCC Student Access Card or an ID card from a Florida community college or public university is required. In addition, any TCC student may use their TCC card to access public university and community college libraries across the state.

After hours, students may use "Ask a Librarian," a statewide reference service easily accessed via the TCC home page. Just go to http://www.tcc.fl.edu and click on "TCC Library" (in the lower right-hand corner).

For hours of operation during final exams, semester breaks, vacation periods, holidays, and the summer academic term, check the special schedules posted in the library and on the library's homepage.

TCC PASSPORT

On the TCC website (http://www.tcc.fl.edu), you can find the latest campus news, upcoming events and activities, registration information, library resources, class schedules, your email account, and links to much more.

The TCC Passport Portal consolidates a number of different TCC services, allowing students to access email, Blackboard, and EagleNet with just one sign-on. The unification of services should make navigating College technologies easier and will also improve communication between TCC students, faculty, and staff.

TCC Passport will post messages and announcements specific to you, and allow TCC to give you the most up-to-date information on your grades, records, and available student resources.

Here are the steps you need to be able to sign on:

Look for the TCC Passport link under the Resources section of the TCC homepage.

Once on the TCC Passport homepage, click on "Sign In" on the menu to the left of the screen. (The text is small, so you may have to look carefully.)

To access TCC Passport, you must enter your user name and password.

Your new TCC Passport **user name** is your **TCC email address** (accessible through the EagleNet Personal Information button).

Your TCC Passport **password** is your current eAccount password. If you need to verify your eAccount password, please access this information through the Personal Information button of the TCC EagleNet system.

You have now accessed your own personal portal page.

What You Can Do—TCC Passport Functions

Notice the Tabs across the top of your TCC Passport page.

TCC Passport—*Portal homepage*

My Schedule—*Register for classes, view your schedule, access Blackboard*

My Success—*Complete My Success modules, view advising information, access transfer manuals*

My Blackboard—*Access the TCC Blackboard system here—view course updates and share information with your instructors*

My Mail—*Your student email, calendar, and contacts*

My Account—*View information related to your TCC finances including tuition and fees and your financial aid award status*

My Records—*View TCC records including your grades, transcript, degree audit, placement scores, contact information, and eAccount information*

My Resources —*Access TCC and community resources—be sure to check this tab regularly, as information will be updated soon*

Clubs/Organizations—*View TCC club and organization web pages and learn more about campus involvement, fitness opportunities, and student volunteer activities*

My TCC—*Under construction, will be a personalized web page allowing you to upload pictures, create a Blog, add to the Wiki, and share tips with other students on your campus experiences; you will be able to save both personal and shared documents through the portal.*

These resources are available while on campus from any computer lab as well as from any computer that has internet access.

CAMPUS DEPARTMENTS THAT CAN ASSIST YOU
Campus Police

(850) 201-6100

Centre Building, 2nd floor

TCC's Police Department was established to support students, faculty, staff, and visitors with their law enforcement and security needs on campus. To achieve its high level of service, TCCPD practices community oriented policing and numerous crime prevention activities. The Department supports the College's mission by providing services accessible to all including motorized escorts and other special services where appropriate.

Campus police officers are certified through the Florida Department of Law Enforcement's Criminal Justice Standards and Training Commission; they have standing to enforce federal, state, and local laws.

The Campus Police Department is on the second floor of the Centre Building, in the heart of campus north of the flagpole. It also houses TCC's Lost and Found, so if you find or lose an item, please contact the Campus Police. Claims require proper identification.

Career Services Center

(850) 201-9970

Student Union, 206

Hours: Monday through Thursday, 8:00 a.m. to 7:00 p.m.

Friday, 8:00 a.m. to 5:00 p.m.

The Career Services Center offers programs and services designed to help students select and manage their careers. Students will find current information on career planning, preparation and placement. The Center also offers computerized career assessment programs, workshops designed to help students transition into the workforce, and the latest information on internships, externships, and permanent employment.

Student Success Center

(850) 201-8440

Student Union, 206

Hours: Monday through Thursday, 8:00 a.m. to 7:00 p.m.

Friday, 8:00 a.m. to 5:00 p.m.

Academic, personal, career, and pre-enrollment counseling is available to all current and prospective TCC students. A counselor or academic advisor helps each student develop his or her educational and career plans before and during initial registration. From then on, faculty advisors help students plan their courses and approve their selections. Counselors are available year-round for consultation, academic advising, career planning, transfer and scholarship information, and assistance with personal concerns.

Personal Counseling Services

(850) 201-8440

Student Union, 206

Hours: Monday through Thursday, 8:00 a.m. to 7:00 p.m.

Friday, 8:00 a.m. to 5:00 p.m.

Personal counseling is available by appointment in TCC's Counseling Department. When calling to request personal services be specific. Tell the person answering the phone that you are seeking personal assistance and not assistance with school or classes. There are two counselors on staff full-time to assist students in this area. A professional counselor helps students explore such personal concerns as anxiety, depression, relationship problems, anger, stress, low self esteem, sexual identity, substance abuse, as well as many other issues.

Disability Support Services (DSS)

(850) 201-8430, voice

(850) 201-8429, TDD

Student Union, 172

The College is deeply committed to ensuring that all programs, services, and facilities are accessible and usable by people with disabilities. Every student is entitled to the maximum benefits of the college experience. However, to qualify for these services a student must provide documentation. Documentation is valid if provided by a medical doctor, psychologist, or other licensed or certified specialist recognized to treat the disability in question. Accommodations and support available to eligible students include note takers, interpreters, extended testing time, adaptive computer labs, and individualized preregistration. While

TCC is responsible for notifying students, faculty, and staff of its available services, students with disabilities must take responsibility for *requesting* the services they need. Lists of these services are included in such TCC publications as the catalog, faculty handbook, brochures, and in the orientation programs for students and staff. DSS provides important support so that students can meet their goals and successfully complete their studies. Trained counselors advise students with disabilities and also act as advocates and liaisons with instructors, staff, and local agencies.

The College is handicap accessible and special parking is available.

Enrollment Services

(850) 201-8555
Student Union, 2nd floor

This office oversees all college records for students, including:

- *Transcripts*
  Students may view their unofficial transcripts on EagleNet. Those wishing to send an official transcript to another party must submit a written request, signed and dated, with a student ID or social security number. This can be done by mail or fax, in person at Enrollment Services, or online via EagleNet for Florida postsecondary schools.

- *Transient Work (Temporary Transfer)*
  Transcripts of all postsecondary work must be submitted to Enrollment Services. Students wishing to take courses at another institution and apply them to a TCC program of study should make this request through Enrollment Services.

- *Updating Student Information*
  It is important that students keep Enrollment Services updated about changes in their personal status (e.g., address, name, program of study, degree choice, and state residency). Such changes can be made by completing a form in Enrollment Services; many can be made online via EagleNet.

Financial Aid

(850) 201-8399
Student Union, 2nd floor

The Financial Aid Office helps students determine their eligibility for financial aid at TCC.

Application Process

First, students should apply for a Personal Identification Number, or PIN, which serves as an electronic signature, at http://www.pin.ed.gov. This will speed up the application process.

Next, students must complete the Free Application for Federal Student Aid online at http://www.fafsa.ed.gov. The application is available in hard copy from the Financial Aid Office, local high schools, or by calling 1-800-4 FED-AID. Hearing-impaired students may call TDD 1-800-730-8913. Students should include TCC on their list of schools designated to receive the FAFSA, as well as TCC's institutional code, which is 001533.

Once the FAFSA is analyzed by the federal government (which usually takes 4 weeks), students will receive an acknowledgment called the Student Aid Report (SAR). Students should retain a copy of their SAR form as it will be needed for future reference. Changes can be made online using the PIN number provided by the government or on the correction pages and be returned to the address on the form. After submitting a change, both the student and TCC will receive a new report containing the update.

To qualify for financial aid, you must be a fully admitted, degree-seeking student and meet the College's standards for academic progress. Transcripts from your previous post-secondary institutions are part of the evaluation process. See Chapter Four on advising for further details about when and how to check on the status of your award.

The following standards of satisfactory progress for financial aid apply to all students:

- Students must maintain a 2.0 GPA.
- Students who fail to maintain a 2.0 cumulative GPA will be placed on Financial Aid Warning Status.
- Students on Warning Status who fail to meet the 2.0 cumulative GPA by the next satisfactory academic progress review period will be ineligible for financial aid.
- Students must complete 67% of classes attempted.
- Attempted hours include all college preparatory courses, withdrawals, incomplete courses, unsatisfactory (failures) grades, and transfer credit hours.
- Students must complete their degree program before attempting more than 150% of the total credit hours required for the program.

Awards

If the SAR form is correct, TCC will receive the information electronically and begin the award process using federal, state, and institutional aid and other resources. This information will be sent to students in an award letter. Financial aid is not distributed until attendance in your classes is verified. In addition, if you drop your classes you may be required to immediately repay the aid awarded for those classes. If you are taking a mixture of Main, A, B, and C classes not all of your financial aid will be awarded at one time. Rather your aid will be distributed as your attendance in each term is verified. Your financial aid award package may be a mixture of loans and grants. Grants do not have to be repaid as long as you complete your program of study. Loans must be repaid over time usually beginning 6 months after leaving school.

Other Types of Financial Assistance

- *Scholarships:* Scholarship information is available online.
- *Veterans' Benefits:* Veterans should contact the Financial Aid Office's VA adviser or call (850) 201-8406.

- *Loans:* Many private loans are also available to students to assist with expenses. Often these loans have unfavorable consequences. See the chapter on money management for further details. To make your transition to college easier, remember to apply early, respond to all correspondence, and be prepared to pay your expenses until you receive your financial aid. Funds may not be available until several weeks after classes start.

Health Services

Health Insurance

While student health insurance is not available through TCC, private insurance companies do provide health care coverage at special rates designed for students. For more information, contact the Campus Life Office in SU 154 or at (850) 201-8420.

Dental Health

Dental cleanings performed by students in the Dental Hygiene program are available for a small fee. Screenings are necessary to receive treatments at TCC's Dental Clinic in DH 142. Call (850) 201-8247.

STUDENT LIFE AT TCC

TCC has much to offer students and there are many benefits to getting involved on your college campus. You'll interact with people of diverse backgrounds and develop better interpersonal skills. What's more, getting involved in student life will prove an excellent networking tool and resume builder. The Campus Life office administers most extracurricular activities at TCC including clubs, organizations, intramurals, student activities, and special events. It also houses Student Volunteerism, the Mentoring Program, and Student Judicial Affairs. Studies show that students who spend more time on campus are more successful. Getting involved in non-class activities at TCC can actually improve your grades.

Student Handbook and Planner

The student handbook is the student's personal guide to everything you need to know about TCC and how you can be successful on campus. It contains information on resources, programs, planning, TCC policies and codes (including the student code of conduct), and provides students with a daily organizer that contains important dates and information to help students stay on track with classes.

Student Volunteerism

(850) 201-6146

Student Union, Room 154

The Office of Student Volunteerism works to impact the community and promote lasting change in Leon, Wakulla, and Gadsden counties via academic enrichment and civic engagement. Students can earn community service hours on their official TCC transcript in the Service-Learning Program. See handbook for further details on how this program works.

Campus Entertainment

(850) 201-8975

Student Union, Room 188

TCC offers a huge selection of recreation, culture, and fun to students via Campus Entertainment. Students are exposed to opportunities from musical and novelty acts, to speakers and holiday trips with the emphasis on diversity. Entertainment is provided both on and off campus and is normally free with a valid TCC student ID. Other events are offered at a reduced rate. In addition, TCC partners with both FSU and FAMU for many off campus activities. Many events that are marketed to FSU and FAMU students are also available to TCC students. Check the local student newspaper, the *TCC Talon*, as well as the *Flambeau/Torch* for information on these events.

Student Government Association (SGA)

(850) 201-8423

Student Union, Room 185

SGA addresses the needs and concerns of the student body as well as the campus budgeting process for student organizations. It serves as the students' voice and their liaison to the TCC administration, campus committees, and other appropriate authorities. Its President, Vice President, Corresponding Secretary, and Scribe are elected by the student body and must receive a majority of votes cast. Their terms of office begin upon election at the end of the spring term and last for 1 year.

Student Organizations

(850) 201-8090

Student Activities Office, Room 188

TCC is home to many student organizations. Students are encouraged to contact club advisors for information. Among the offerings are:

Ambassadors for Christ (AFC)

Art Club

Baptist Collegiate Ministries

Black Student Union

Brain Bowl

College Democrats

College Republicans

Eagle Business Society

Encore

Extreme Sport Racing

FG-LSAMPSEMCSC (Florida Georgia-Lewis Stokes Alliance for Minority Participation in Science, Engineering, Mathematics, and Computer Science Club)

Haitian Culture Club

Hispanic/Latino Student Union

Honors Club

International Student Organization

MacPac Graphic Design Club

Model United Nations

Outdoor Recreation Community Volunteer Club

Phi Theta Kappa

PRIDE

RASO (Returning Adult Student Organization)

Sigma Phi Alpha

Speech and Debate Team—Forensics

Student Ambassador Program

Student American Dental Hygiene Association (SADHA)

TCC Chapter of the NAACP

TCC Dance Company

LIFETIME SPORTS COMPLEX

(850) 201-8709 or 201-8093

Lifetime Sports Complex, Room 106

The Lifetime Sports Fitness Facility is a great place to work out, meet new people, and participate in informal recreational activities. It houses the fitness facility, gym, a wide variety of aerobics classes, the campus intramurals program, the athletic department, academic recreation classes, and department office.

The fitness facility offers a variety of resistance and cardiovascular machines as well as free weights. The recreation gym is open to informal recreation. Hours of operation may vary by semester. Admission is free with a valid TCC ID card.

Intramural Sports

Students, faculty, and staff can participate in over 16 team and individual sports and events, all free of charge.

Eagle Adventures

(850) 201-8710

Lifetime Sports 105

Eagle Adventures is a TCC campus recreation program committed to offering a variety of affordable adventure sports and outdoor recreation opportunities to students that promote health, fitness, and wellness. Throughout each semester, Eagle Adventures offers outdoor activities that are inclusive of all levels and abilities; however, not all trips are suitable for everyone. Contact Robin Meeks for more details.

MUSIC PROGRAMS

(850) 201-6070

The *Tallahassee Civic Chorale* is a group of nonaudition singers that performs in community settings. *Illuminare* is TCC's show choir. The *Capital City Band* performs at graduation and other community events. The *TCC Jazz Band* is a nonaudition group focusing on stage band music and performing on and off campus. The *Big Bend Community Orchestra* consists of community members and TCC students. Some of these groups are also available as credit classes. Check with your advisor for details.

Open Mic

(850) 201-8047

Shauna Smith

Open Mic is an ongoing showcase for talented TCC student performers. It provides a stage for those who need one. This series is a nonjudged forum that welcomes and encourages a diverse array of talent. Several sessions are scheduled each fall and spring semester. Performances must be previewed prior to Open Mic dates.

TCC FORENSICS AND THEATER

(850) 201-8037

John Schultz

The championship *TCC Speech and Debate* team competes nationally and has an outstanding record of success, while its theater program presents several shows each season featuring a director from the faculty or a noted community artist. Students are encouraged to participate in all areas of production: acting, stage management, running crews, set, props, lighting, sound, and costumes.

Thanks to the generous support of TCC's Student Government Association, all *TheatreTCC!* productions are free to students, faculty, and staff. Scholarships are available for students who contribute artistically in a substantial way to the program.

SUMMARY

Becoming acquainted with TCC is vital to taking advantage of the campus's many resources. Chances are you'll need to know the location of these important offices during your time here.

TCC provides wide-ranging opportunities for students to get involved in social and academic activities. You'll find assistance with reading, writing, and math in the Learning

Commons, while the Career Services Center, computer labs, Student Success Center, and Library offer state-of-the-art support for your needs. Student life is teeming with clubs and events, so there's something for everyone.

Take advantage of what the College has to offer and get involved! It will enrich your experience as a TCC student.

COLLEGE INFORMATION HUNT

1. When was the last day to cancel your registration and receive a refund?

2. When is the last day to withdraw from a course and receive a "W" grade?

3. When is the last day to withdraw from the college?

4. What English class can you take after ENC1101?

5. What is Tallahassee Community College's web address?

6. List the three alternative instructional methods (other than the traditional classroom) used at TCC.

7. What is the beginning and ending date for the B accelerated term?

8. When is the final exam for a MWF 12:20 class?

9. What is Tallyscript?

10. What is your instructor's name?

11. Where do you register for classes?

12. What program do you use to access your online classes?

13. How many learning commons are there on campus?

14. Which department do you go to if you need help with test taking?

15. What item is required in order to access anything you need on campus?

16. What are the hours for the Lifetime Sports Complex?

17. What intramural sports are offered at TCC?

18. How many credits are required to receive an A.A.?

19. What does CLAST stand for?

20. What is the name of the president of TCC?

Chapter 2

Diversity

on the College Campus and Beyond

LEARNING OBJECTIVES

By the end of this chapter you should be able to:

Define diversity

Explain the types of diversity on TCC's campus

Know why diversity is important

Understand some vocabulary words relating to diversity

Since 1966, Tallahassee Community College (TCC) has provided top-notch instruction to the citizens of Leon, Gadsden, and Wakulla Counties. The publication *Community College Week* ranked TCC 14th in the nation in awarding Associate in Arts degrees. For a 2-year institution, we have an unusually large number of students from other parts of Florida and the U.S.—indeed, from all over the world—thus we have students with diverse backgrounds and experiences. Thanks to TCC's outstanding disability support services, for instance, we have and are able to provide an education for many students with special needs. We have a thriving global education program that attracts many students from abroad. And, since we reach out to encourage diverse groups to enroll, we have large numbers of returning adult students, nonnative English speakers, and students with different religious backgrounds, career goals, and sexual preferences. Fully 40% of our student body is made up of people of color. We're proud that TCC awards the highest percentage of A.A. degrees to African Americans and people with disabilities of Florida's 28 community colleges. TCC has committed the necessary resources to help this exceptionally diverse population to succeed in college and beyond.

DIVERSITY IS REAL

Diversity is defined as the condition of being **diverse**. But how do we define diverse? It is the act of differing from one another: being unlike in qualities or elements. Diversity is the inclusion of people from different races or cultures in a group or organization.

Another word for *diversity* is *difference*. Differences do not make any particular group inferior or superior. Differences aren't deficits; they're just differences. Look around your classroom, place of employment, or the places where you do business. You'll notice people of a wide range of races, genders, ethnicities, ages, cultures, religions, politics, socio-economic levels, and sexual orientations. It's common to be proud of our identity and to look around for those who share that identity. The challenge is to be able to look at the world from the standpoint of those who differ from us and accept others without **prejudice**.

Campuses, workplaces—truly, the entire nation—are becoming more diverse, so gaining an understanding and appreciation of diversity will help you succeed. Understanding yourself and taking pride in your unique qualities is the first step. *Self-knowledge* includes a grasp of your values, personality, interests, and talents. This chapter challenges you to examine and take pride in yourself while respecting the differences of others.

WHY IS DIVERSITY IMPORTANT?

Having an understanding and appreciation of the concept of diversity can help you succeed both at school and at work. Recognizing that not all people are going to be like you and allowing them to be who they are is part of the growing process. This acceptance also helps to prevent discrimination and evens the playing field for all peoples. Here are some benefits you can gain from understanding the need for acceptance of those who are different from you in some way:

Gain Skills in Critical Thinking

Critical thinking requires identifying different views, questioning each one, getting more information, and then constructing your own reasonable outlook. Critical thinking is an *expected* outcome of higher education. Many of your assignments are designed to teach these skills. Whether you're writing an essay for an English class, participating in a discussion of U.S. history, or conducting a laboratory experiment, critical thinking skills help you succeed.

Critical thinking also promotes good solutions to workplace problems and challenges. A business manager, for instance, must build his or her employees into a team, and critical thinking results in improved understanding of others and, therefore, better problem-solving skills. What's more, to stay competitive, businesses must find creative ways to build and provide quality products and customer service. Critical thinking skills help people work together, come up with good ideas, and boost their business to success.

Gain the Ability to Network with and Learn from Others

In college, you have the opportunity to learn from professors and other students who are quite different from you. You may have professors with personalities and teaching styles you've never seen before. Further, you may encounter a professor who is from a different country or religious background or who suffers from a disability. Therefore, your success will depend on understanding the differences between you and adapting to them. Each student in your classes will also come from a different perspective and have valuable ideas to add to the class.

It is through networking with others that most people find a job. You are likely to find a job through someone you know such as a college professor, a student in one of your classes, a community member, or a referral from a previous employer. Once you have the job, you will gain proficiency by learning from others. The best managers are open to learning from others and helping different people to work together as a team. No matter how educated or experienced you become, you can always learn from others. Bill Cosby once told a graduating class at Washington University, "Don't ever think you know more than the person mopping the floor." Every person has a different view of the world and has important ideas to share.

Improve Your Interpersonal Skills

A popular Native American proverb is that you cannot understand another person until you have walked a few miles in their moccasins. Being able to understand different perspectives on life will help you to improve your personal relationships. Good interpersonal skills bring joy to our personal relationships and are very valuable in the workplace. The Secretary of Labor's Commission on Achieving Necessary Skills (SCANS) identifies having good interpersonal skills as one of the five critical competencies needed in the workplace. Workers need to work effectively in teams, teach others, serve customers, exercise leadership, negotiate to arrive at a decision, and work well with cultural diversity. Efficiency and profits in any industry depend on good interpersonal skills and how well workers can provide customer service.

Learn to Be Flexible and Adapt to New Situations

These two qualities are necessary for dealing with the rapid change that is taking place in our society today. We learn these qualities by successfully facing personal challenges. If you are a single parent, you have learned to be flexible in managing time and resources. If you served in the military overseas, you have learned to adapt to a different culture. If you are a new college student, you are probably learning how to be independent and manage your own life. Flexibility is a valuable skill in the workplace. Today's employers want workers who can adapt, be flexible, and solve problems.

Develop Cultural Awareness

Cultural awareness is valuable in your personal life and in the workplace. In your personal life, you can have a wider variety of satisfying personal relationships. You can enjoy people from different cultural backgrounds and travel to different countries. In a global economy, cultural awareness is increasingly important. Tuning in to cultural differences can open up business opportunities. For example, many companies are discovering that the buying power of minorities is significant. They are developing advertising campaigns to sell products to Asians, Latinos, African Americans, and other groups. Companies now understand that cultural awareness is important in international trade. American car manufacturers could not understand why the Chevy Nova was not selling well in Latin America. In Spanish, "No va" means "It doesn't go" or "It doesn't run." Kentucky Fried Chicken found out that "Finger-lickin' good" translates as "Eat your fingers off" in Chinese! Being familiar with the culture and language of different countries is necessary for successful international business.

UNDERSTANDING DIVERSITY

There are more than *6 billion* people in the world today, and that number is growing all the time, so it's vital to understand the harmful effects of stereotyping in order to improve our appreciation of diversity. **Stereotyping** is making the assumption that every member of a group is alike. For instance, a tall African American woman studying at TCC was constantly dealing with the assumption that she must be attending college to play basketball. Actually, she was very academically oriented and not athletic in the least. Despite this obvious wrong conclusion, all of us use stereotypes to understand people who are different from ourselves. Why? There are many reasons:

- We tend to look for patterns in our search for understanding.
- We're often unable or unwilling to obtain all the information we need to judge others fairly.
- We often learn as children to fear people who are different.
- It's a short-cut to making sense of the world, requiring little thought or investment.
- The media promotes stereotypes. Movies, magazines, and advertisements rely heavily on them. These stereotypes are often used as the basis of humor, such as the reliance in comedy routines on people who are overweight.

The trouble with stereotypes is that we don't get to know people for their own sake. Not all members of a particular culture, ethnic group, or gender are alike. When we make assumptions about a group, then we treat everyone in that group in the same way. Thus stereotypes can lead to prejudice and discrimination. For instance, due to being a stereotypical object of comedy, people who are overweight may find it harder to get a job.

Today sociologists and psychologists accept the idea of *cultural relativity*, in which the traits of cultures, ethnic groups, genders, and sexual preferences are viewed as different but equally valuable and worthy of respect. Such differences can enrich our worldview and promote better understanding and relationships among people and nations.

SUMMARY

It's very important to understand what diversity is and how it can help you become a successful learner. Stereotypes only hurt us, since they prevent our getting to know others as unique individuals. Remember: diversity means differences, not deficits. TCC is a diverse campus, offering many opportunities to celebrate diversity.

The following exercises will help you to further understand the concept of diversity and will provide examples of how diversity works in the world around you.

FIND SOMEONE WHO . . .

Walk around the classroom and find someone who fits each description. Have the person write his or her name on the appropriate line.

Shares a favorite hobby

Father or mother grew up in a bilingual family

Parents or grandparents were born outside the United States

Speaks a language besides English

Is the first one in the family to attend college

Enjoys the same sports

Knows someone who has died of AIDS

Has a friend or relative who is gay, lesbian, or bisexual

Has a disability they have had to overcome

Is struggling financially to attend college

Has children

Is a single parent

Has your same major

Was born in the same year as yourself

Attended your high school

Moved here from out of state

Has been in the military

Has participated on an athletic team

Can play a musical instrument or sing

Has played in a band

EXPLORING DIVERSITY

1. Diversity is another word for difference.

    a. True

    b. False

2. Having an understanding of diversity **will not** help you succeed at work or at school.

    a. True

    b. False

3. Socioeconomic standing is an example of diversity.

    a. True

    b. False

4. Diversity is important, for it will:

    a. Develop cultural awareness

    b. Provide support for your belief in the superiority of a race

    c. Learn to adapt to new situations and belief systems

    d. Identify the failing of certain cultural beliefs

    e. Improve your interpersonal skills

5. Match the correct term with the associated definition.

    _____ 1. Race   _____ 5. Stereotype

    _____ 2. Ethnicity   _____ 6. Prejudice

    _____ 3. Culture   _____ 7. Discrimination

    _____ 4. Sexism   _____ 8. Racism

    a. When people are denied rights or opportunities due to their differences; based on class or category rather than individual merit

    b. An individual, race, or ethnic group holds a negative attitude or perception of another race. Prejudice based on race.

    c. Prior, often incomplete judgment of a person, group, or idea. A negative judgment or opinion formed beforehand or without knowledge or examination of the facts.

    d. Behavior, customs, language, and values shared by members of a group.

    e. Generalizations that express conventional or biased ideas about people of a certain group.

    f. Sense of belonging to a particular culture and sharing its beliefs, ceremonies, and other traditions.

    g. Groups seen as different due to physical characteristics, nationality, or geographic location.

    h. Negative attitude or perception based on sex.

6. What influences our assumptions about people?

   a. Media
   b. Family and friends
   c. School
   d. Personal experiences
   e. Hearsay and gossip
   f. All but E
   g. All of the above

7. To ensure its technology staff is young and modern, a company regularly discards applications from those whose education and/or employment history shows them to be older than 45. This is an example of:

   a. Stereotype
   b. Discrimination
   c. Opinion
   d. Prejudice

8. "All Asians are smart." This statement is an example of:

   a. Stereotype
   b. Discrimination
   c. Opinion
   d. Prejudice

9. LaShanda's parents refuse to allow her to date a Jewish boy under any circumstances. Their reasons are all similar to: Jews are more willing to use shady practices to get what they want; Jews don't care what happens to anyone but their own kind. This is an example of:

   a. Stereotype
   b. Discrimination
   c. Opinion
   d. Prejudice
   e. Racism

10. Explain what diversity means to you.

Provide at least five examples for each of the following.

11. In what ways is the college diverse?

12. What positive value can this diversity bring to your education, relationships within the community, and work?

13. We are all prone to making assumptions about other people but we need to make every effort to base our judgments on fact and not opinion, myth, or stereotypes. What influences our assumptions?

STEREOTYPES

Stereotypes are not only harmful in their own right; they do damage by fostering prejudice and discrimination. Refer to the definitions located in your textbook to assist you in determining whether the following scenarios are examples of:

Discrimination (D), Opinion (O), Prejudice (P), Racism (R), Sexism(S)

SCENARIO	D, O, P, R, OR S?
A young Hispanic male being told a job is filled when it isn't.	
Asian people are always good in school and in math.	
An Asian girl telling her black friend that her new hairstyle isn't as nice as the one she had before.	
A white Catholic female student facing the hostility and negative opinion of her parents toward her Jewish boyfriend due to his religious beliefs.	
A black Muslim woman who wears a hijab (head-scarf) is subject to racial slurs and taunts at work.	
A woman employed by a company in the same job position as a male colleague with the same job experience but receiving a lower salary.	
An advertisement for the local accounting firm depicting the accountant as a thin, mousey looking man wearing thick glasses and a cardigan sweater.	
To ensure its technology staff is young and modern, a company regularly discards applications from those whose education and/or employment history shows them to be older than 45.	
Blondes always want to have fun.	
A young man from a poor southern town has earned a full academic scholarship to a prestigious northern college. He is being ostracized and ridiculed for his accent and lack of money at the college he attends.	
Burning of churches because they serve the black community.	
A young white woman tells an elderly Hispanic coworker that Steven King is a better writer than Aldo Alvarez (a Hispanic author).	

Chapter 3

Motivation, Personal Responsibility, and Locus of Control—Moving Me to Success

LEARNING OBJECTIVES

By the end of this chapter you should be able to:

Define motivation, personal responsibility and locus of control
Identify and list characteristics of intrinsic and extrinsic motivation
List methods for improving motivation

WHAT IS MOTIVATION?

Motivation is your inspiration and commitment to achieve a goal—whether academic, professional, or personal. The strength and depth of your motivation has a strong influence on how well you perform in school and at work. Keep in mind that motivation is not the same as determination. You may be very determined to complete your Associate in Arts, Associate in Science, or Bachelor's degree, but that is not the same as your motivation for doing so. Instead, ask yourself, "Why do I want a degree?" That identifies the source of your motivation: lots of opportunity, a good income, public service, desire for travel, or to settle in a small town or city. Whatever the source of your drive, it sustains your determination and inspiration to study, learn, and succeed in your academic efforts.

There are two types of motivation: intrinsic and extrinsic. An *extrinsically motivated* student is one who is inspired to learn for external reasons, such as pleasing family, friends, a teacher, or an employer. The student may perform well to achieve a reward, compete for a high grade, or avoid a negative consequence. To be *intrinsically motivated*, your reasons and inspirations are internal; the motivations come from within you. To be intrinsically motivated to learn means that learning satisfies your personal goals, desires, or values. If you are intrinsically motivated, you will be more likely to earn high grades, retain important concepts, complete assigned tasks, persist in your efforts to learn, and put effort into your academic endeavors.

In both the workplace and the classroom, you need to take personal responsibility for your motivation. This is important when trying to reach both your academic and employment goals. Employers value employees who have high performance standards, are intrinsically motivated to perform tasks, and actively seek out opportunities to improve their skills and knowledge.

IMPROVING YOUR MOTIVATION TO LEARN

Step 1: Become an Intrinsically Motivated Individual

To be truly successful in life, remember that only you can motivate yourself to learn and study. *You* are in charge of your life, your goals, and your learning.

Step 2: Believe in Yourself

Believing in yourself is crucial to successfully meeting your goals! You *can* succeed—with determination, hard work, and commitment. Students who expect to succeed in their academic endeavors will be more motivated to learn and be successful in learning. If you find you need assistance with your schoolwork, talk to your instructor or visit the Learning Commons. The Learning Commons can provide assistance in math, writing, and reading. The Computer Labs can assist you in using the computer and understanding basic office software.

Step 3: Realize Success Takes Personal Effort and Commitment

Your success is directly related to the amount of effort you put into achieving your goals. The more effort you give, the more likely you are to achieve. This means *you* must take responsibility for your successes and failures. If you do poorly on a test due to lack of effort don't blame the instructor or anyone else.

Step 4: Identify *Why* You Are Attending College

If you're not certain of your reasons for attending college, make an appointment with a counselor to determine what your reasons are and how TCC can help you succeed. Find out exactly what to do to achieve your personal and academic goals. What classes are required for an A.A. or A.S. degree? Is there a specific order in which courses must be taken? How long will it take to complete your education? How much will it cost? Are you eligible for financial aid? Are there specific courses required when transferring from TCC to Florida State University, Florida A&M University, or another 4-year college of your choice? Answering these questions will help you identify your academic goals and will also help you to complete them in a timely manner.

Step 5: Make Learning Your Top Priority

Don't let your social life interfere with your main task of performing well in school and earning your degree or certificate. Use the planning and time management skills you learn in this class to help prioritize your tasks. You may wish to refer to the chapter on time management for suggestions on how to make the best use of your time. If you find you have difficulty concentrating on your studies, try to determine what's causing the difficulty and take steps to eliminate the problem(s). If you would like to talk to someone about your personal or academic situation, TCC has excellent guidance counselors.

Step 6: Identify Your Preferred Study and Learning Environment

Do you prefer studying at home or at the library? Do you prefer more self directed learning, as in an online course, or the traditional environment of a classroom with an instructor and other students? Knowing the answer to these questions will help you choose the learning environment that best suits your learning style and motivation. More about learning environments can be found in the chapter on learning styles, which is discussed later in this course.

Step 7: Set Realistic Long- and Short-Term Goals

Setting realistic goals is crucial to your success and maintaining your motivation to learn. Review the chapter on goals for how to set long- and short-term goals.

Step 8: Reward Yourself

Congratulate and reward yourself when you study hard and do well. Start with rewarding yourself for small goals such as studying for an hour or completing a set number of questions. Gradually increase the amount of work/time needed to obtain the reward. Be sure to make the reward something you enjoy, such as going to the movies, hiking, or playing a video game.

Step 9: Make Friends with People Who Are Optimistic, Positive Thinkers

The people around you can really affect your attitudes, motivation, and outlook on life. By associating with people who share your values, you will find understanding and encouragement in the pursuit of your goals, just as you will be able to return them. On the other hand, if you frequently associate with family, friends, or coworkers who are pessimistic or even try to discourage or hinder you, you will find that your motivation slowly begins to dissolve. Over time, you may watch yourself drifting further and further away from your goals.

Do you find that you have a negative outlook on life? You can change this! At the end of each day, list three good things that happened. It can be as simple as getting a good grade on an assignment, meeting someone new, or enjoying a meal. Reflecting on your day in this manner can help you focus on the good instead of the bad things in life.

WHAT IS LOCUS OF CONTROL?

Locus of control is your personal belief regarding what controls your behavior: the factors and personal experience that you believe cause your success or failure in meeting your goals. When college students have a strong *internal locus of control*, they attribute their success to their own efforts, skills, knowledge, and abilities. They believe they are in charge of their own academic destiny. A student with internal locus of control is more likely to seek out information and assistance. He or she will have good study habits, a positive academic attitude, and the ability to learn from experience. When students with a strong internal locus of control perform poorly academically, they can connect it to something they did not understand or accomplish. They will then figure out what needs to be done next time so the problem does not recur, such as seeking assistance or changing their study strategy. A strong internal locus of control is directly related to your chance of success, both academically and in the workforce.

In contrast, students with a strong *external locus of control* do not feel they are in control of their successes and failures. This type of individual attributes success and failure to outside sources: luck, fate, parents, roommates, coworkers, or teachers. These students are much less likely to make the effort needed to learn, because they do not see a relationship between the amount of time they study and their grades. Instead, if they perform poorly, they blame the instructor or another outside factor, such as having been sleepy during the test. Since students with an external locus of control believe they are not in control of their lives, they are more likely to experience anxiety. They are also less likely to seek assistance from their instructors, counselors, tutors, or other academic support resources.

PERSONAL RESPONSIBILITY

Protecting and nurturing your health and emotional well-being by communicating your needs assertively in your relationships is a part of taking self-responsibility for your actions. Other important parts of self-responsibility include:

- Acknowledging that you are solely responsible for the choices in your life.
- Accepting that you are responsible for what you choose to feel or think.
- Accepting that you choose the direction for your life.
- Accepting that you cannot blame others for the choices you have made.

- Recognizing that you are your best cheerleader; it is not reasonable or healthy for you to depend on others to make you feel good about yourself.
- Recognizing that as you enter adulthood and maturity, you determine how your self-esteem will develop.
- Taking preventive health oriented steps of structuring your life with time management, stress management, confronting fears, and burnout prevention.
- Taking an honest inventory of your strengths, abilities, talents, virtues, and positive points.

CONSIDER THE FOLLOWING SCENARIO

Bill is a freshman at TCC. He works 30 hours a week and is taking 15 semester hours. He is having difficulty getting to class on time, so his professors are annoyed with him for coming in late and disturbing the class. He isn't doing very well on his assignments, and most of the time he doesn't know what's going on in class. Bill thinks his professors are being unreasonable—after all, he has a very busy schedule with work, school, and having a personal life! It isn't his fault that he has to work so much. He would be performing better in his biology class if the instructor made it more interesting and would be flexible about the due dates. He thinks that maybe college isn't for him. He really likes history and computers, but his parents want him to major in biology.

Do you think Bill has an understanding of personal responsibility and how it affects him?? What can you say about his level of motivation? What advice would you have for Bill?

SUMMARY

Proper *motivation* is critical to achieving your goals, including academic success. Identifying what motivates you will help you perform well in your studies. Increasing your understanding of your goals, being ***intrinsically motivated***, understanding ***personal responsibility***, and making your goals your own can turn weak motivations into strong motivations, and make strong motivations into solid convictions!

EXERCISE: MOTIVATION

In your own words, define motivation.

_____

_____

_____

_____

Now that you understand the meaning of intrinsic motivation, take a moment to identify three intrinsic motivations for why you wish to learn more by taking college level courses or obtain a college degree.

1. _____

_____

_____

2. _____

_____

_____

3. _____

_____

_____

Chapter 4

Ready, Set—GOAL!

LEARNING OBJECTIVES

By the end of this chapter you should be able to:

Identify and list short- and long-term goals

Explain how to set personal, social, career, and academic goals

Identify reachable goals

Explain the importance of setting specific, measurable goals, and for achieving those goals

Explain the role of values and personal commitment to successfully achieving goals

Discuss how goal-setting can improve your problem solving skills and sense of personal responsibility

WHAT ARE GOALS?

Goals are objectives that you want to achieve. We all want more in our lives, whether changing a bad habit or getting an education or a better job. But simply wishing for change won't make things happen. You must take charge and set goals to move forward in life.

Goals should be **specific, measurable, attainable, realistic,** and **timely.** Setting goals is a process of identifying the aims and achievements you consider vital to fulfill. By making goals as concrete and specific as possible, you can solidify your commitment and identify the steps you must take to successfully achieve them.

First, you need such a strong desire to achieve a goal that you are willing to work hard and sacrifice in order to achieve it. What would you sacrifice to reach your goals? Take a moment to identify some of your goals. Don't worry if you think they are too ambitious and difficult to achieve. Later in this chapter, you'll learn strategies to stay focused and break long-term goals into smaller, more manageable ones. As you identify your goals, ask yourself if they are consistent with your values, characteristics, abilities, and determination. Equally important whether or not they are ethical. Also remember that goals must come with some flexibility. If not, when an obstacle arises, and it will, you will be unable to complete your goal and will lose focus.

WHY SET GOALS?

People with goals achieve more than those without them. It's that simple. Think of successful people whom you especially respect. Could they have succeeded without setting goals? What goals do you imagine they set for themselves?

A goal by itself is never enough. Without a plan for how you will achieve your goal, it is little more than wishful thinking. Fulfilling your goals and dreams takes true commitment and purpose. It isn't easy, but once you know what you want to do, you will be able to accept the demands and challenges to meet your goals head on.

To stay motivated and achieve your dreams in a timely manner, you must identify long- and short-term goals. First, clearly identify a goal you want to achieve. Then plan how you will go about achieving it. When you have identified a specific goal, it is much easier to create a plan with the steps necessary to achieve it, assess your progress toward meeting it, and succeed in accomplishing it. Once again, allow for flexibility in your goal. Have a back-up plan in place in case a life event occurs which throws your goal off track.

LONG- AND SHORT-TERM GOALS

Long- and short-term goals are vital tools in measuring success and keeping yourself motivated. *Long-term goals* focus on what you plan to achieve in the next few years. They can be personal, social, career, or academic. A long-term goal, such as earning an A.A. degree or saving for a down payment on a house, takes a long time to accomplish. To achieve a long-term goal, you'll need to create a plan and identify all the short-term goals that, step by step, will take you where you want to be.

To ensure success, it is important to identify as many of the short-term goals necessary to accomplish a long-term goal.

A *short-term goal* can be measured easily and accomplished in a relatively short time: an hour, a day, a week, or a semester. Breaking down a problem or goal into small parts is always the best way to tackle it. Have you ever been overwhelmed by a problem, not knowing where to begin to

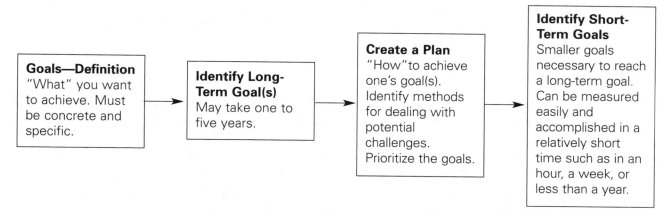

solve it? By dividing a challenge into smaller, more manageable tasks or goals, you can see what needs to be done, keep your motivation high, and prevent procrastination.

Here's an example. Sam's car broke down and he needs a new one, but he doesn't have the $500 necessary for a down payment. Rather than feel overwhelmed by the task of coming up with $500, Sam could set a short-term goal of putting aside $25 a week for 5 months to save enough for a down payment. In the meantime, of course, he'll have to sacrifice his convenience by catching the bus, walking, riding a bicycle, or arranging rides with friends.

Ellen, a business major, thought she was going to graduate (long-term goal) at the end of the spring semester. She hadn't had her courses reviewed or seen a counselor (short-term goals) yet, but didn't think there would be a problem. She went to many interviews during the spring semester and was offered a well-paying job at a bank (long-term goal) upon graduation. Ellen was extremely excited about graduating and having obtained an excellent job opportunity right out of college! However, on doing her graduation check, Ellen was

TYPES OF GOALS

Career Goals	• Write a cover letter • Improve public speaking abilities • Learn a new job skill
Academic Goals	• Increase GPA to 3.0 for this semester • Earn A.A. in _____ (month) of _____(year) • Meet with math study group once a week
Personal Goals	• Lose 10 pounds • Make an appointment with a counselor for next week • Sign up for a Monday, Wednesday, Friday exercise class
Social Goals	• Get involved in student government or volunteer work at TCC • Spend one evening each week on an activity with my spouse/ loved one • Develop better communication skills by taking a course on Tuesday evenings

absolutely horrified to find she was going to be one class short. She wasn't ready to graduate and was going to have to turn down a wonderful job because a degree was needed before employment.

Related Goals

As you learn more about goals, you will find that many of your *career, academic, personal,* and *social* goals will relate closely to each other. Let's look at what happened with Tom. He began school with: (a) a *personal goal* of working in a field that he found interesting and motivating, (b) an *academic goal* of getting a degree in Computer Science, and (c) a *career goal* of working as a programmer for a local computer company.

Each of these goals had a relationship to the others. While Tom had never done any programming, he'd always thoroughly enjoyed computers and technology. His college counselor recommended that he take some computer programming courses to decide if programming was truly the best choice for him. After doing so, Tom concluded that this was not the part of technology that he enjoyed! What he really preferred was setting up computers and home entertainment systems, trouble-shooting problems, and teaching people how to use electronics in their home or how to use personal devices, such as smart phones. As you can see, this career goal was very different from computer programming.

Although Tom had entered school with a career goal, his experiences and exposure to programming made him reassess his choice. His personal goal did not change, but he realized he needed to reevaluate his academic and career goals. After discussions with his counselor, Tom changed his career goal to obtaining the skills and knowledge necessary to start his own business. His business would be installing and maintaining home computer and entertainment systems and tutoring his customers on home and personal mobile technology. Tom's new academic goal then became earning a Bachelor's degree in business, with a focus on entrepreneurship.

Tom also found that his social and career goals overlapped. Since he would be working with customers on a daily basis, he realized that he would need to develop his communication and interpersonal skills. Thus Tom identified social goals to fully

meet his career goal. After speaking with his counselor and friends, he decided to join a public speaking club on campus.

ETHICAL AND PERSONAL GOALS

Ethical goals demonstrate the quality of your character, an understanding of right from wrong, and the rules that govern us, both professionally and personally. All goals, no matter why you set them, should fall within this category. The box below outlines for you how to measure whether your goals are ethical or not.

ETHICAL GOALS DEMONSTRATE:

- **Caring.** Show your consideration, caring, and empathy to others while striving to achieve your goals.

- **Fairness.** Your goals should enable you to treat everyone fairly. Don't take credit for other people's work under any circumstances. Play by the rules; rules are made for everyone!

- **Respect.** Goals should show that you respect diverse beliefs and lifestyles.

- **Responsibility.** Always take responsibility for your own actions and be willing to pay the consequences of your mistakes.

- **Trustworthiness.** Your goals should reflect your beliefs while demonstrating your honesty and sincerity.

Make your goals your own. Each of your goals should be driven and identified by your values, beliefs, passions, and dreams. They should reflect your *personal values.* In other words, goals should be important, highly desirable, and strongly motivating. Why do you want to achieve a particular goal? Whether you want to learn more about technology, develop an exercise program, spend more time with family, or complete a degree, you need goals that are relevant and meaningful. And you are the best one to identify your strengths, weaknesses, and dreams—as well as the steps to maximize your chances of success. Goals identified by your family, friends, or employer will not help you find meaning in life or joy in your achievements.

SMART GOALS

When setting goals it is often helpful to think of them in relation to the acronym **SMART**. **SMART** is explained in the following way:

Specific—A specific goal has a much greater chance of being accomplished than a general goal. To set a specific goal you must answer the six "W" questions:

*Who: Who is involved?
*What: What do I want to accomplish?
*Where: Identify a location.
*When: Establish a timeframe.
*Which: Identify requirements and constraints.
*Why: Specific reasons, purpose, or benefits of accomplishing the goal.

EXAMPLE: A general goal would be, "Get in shape." But a specific goal would say, "Join a health club and work out 3 days a week."

Measurable— Establish concrete criteria for measuring progress toward the attainment of each goal you set. When you measure your progress, you stay on track, reach your target dates, and experience the exhilaration of achievement that spurs you on to continued effort required to reach your goal.

To determine if your goal is measurable, ask questions such as How much? How many? How will I know when it is accomplished?

Attainable —When you identify goals that are most important to you, you begin to figure out ways you can make them come true. You develop the attitudes, abilities, skills, and financial capacity to reach them. You begin seeing previously overlooked opportunities to bring yourself closer to the achievement of your goals.

You can attain most any goal you set when you plan your steps wisely and establish a timeframe that allows you to carry out those steps. Goals that may have seemed far away and out of reach eventually move closer and become attainable, not because your goals shrink, but because you grow and expand to match them. When you list your goals you build your self-image. You see yourself as worthy of these goals, and develop the traits and personality that allow you to possess them.

Realistic—To be realistic, a goal must represent an objective toward which you are both *willing* and *able* to work. A goal can be both high and realistic; you are the only one who can decide just how high your goal should be. But be sure that every goal represents substantial progress. A high goal is frequently easier to reach than a low one because a low goal exerts low motivational force. Some of the hardest jobs you ever accomplished actually seem easy simply because they were a labor of love.

Your goal is probably realistic if you truly *believe* that it can be accomplished. Additional ways to know if your goal is realistic is to determine if you have accomplished anything similar in the past or ask yourself what conditions would have to exist to accomplish this goal.

Timely—A goal should be grounded within a timeframe. With no timeframe tied to it there's no sense of urgency. If you want to lose 10 lbs, when do you want to lose it by? "Someday" won't work. But if you anchor it within a timeframe, "by May 1st," then you've set your unconscious mind into motion to begin working on the goal.

T can also stand for **Tangible**—A goal is tangible when you can experience it with one of the senses; that is, taste, touch, smell, sight, or hearing. When your goal is tangible you have a better chance of making it specific and measurable and thus attainable.

EXAMPLE GOAL SETTING CHART

"An unwritten want is a wish, a dream, a never happen. The day you put your goal in writing is the day it becomes a commitment that will change your life. Are you ready?"

—TOM HOPKINS

Setting goals is a means of identifying and plotting how you are going to achieve your aims in life. By writing down your goals you are committing yourself to accomplishing them; therefore, make sure that your goals are important to YOU. In the above section you were shown how to go about carefully selecting your goals and choosing the best possible methods to achieve them. Below is an example chart for semester goals and strategies set by a college student. Notice how the goals listed below are realistic, measurable, and can be reviewed. *Keep in mind that this is an example list; your own lists may have completely different goals and will most likely be far more extensive.*

GOAL #1: EARN A 3.50 GPA FOR THIS SEMESTER.

Strategies for Achieving Goal #1

1. Study at least 3 hours 5 days a week. Tuesdays and Thursdays I will go to the library immediately after my 1:00 class.

2. Organize study groups to make sure I am fully prepared for exams. Make sure to meet at least 3 times before an exam.

3. Meet with each of my professors at least 2 times this semester. I will go prepared to ask questions about exams at least 1 week in advance.

GOAL #2: CHOOSE A MAJOR BY THE MIDDLE OF MY THIRD SEMESTER.

Strategies for Achieving Goal #2

1. Examine personal interests and possible career choices. Make a list of at least 5 majors that spark interest and possible careers that could be formed out of each major. I will make sure to have the list completed by the beginning of my third semester of college.

2. Make an appointment at the Career Development Center to take their computerized DISCOVER assessment which helps to define interests and abilities in order to give better direction toward choosing a major.

3. I will meet with my academic advisor at least 3 times this semester to help make decisions about choosing a major. I'm going to be sure to discuss major requirements.

Now that you have seen how to do it, try it for yourself.

Goal #1:
Strategies for Achieving Goal #1

1. _____

2. _____

3. _____

Goal #2:
Strategies for Achieving Goal #2

1. _____

2. _____

3. _____

STRATEGIES FOR SUCCESSFULLY ACHIEVING GOALS

Even when your goals are specific, concrete, and clear, you may still find it difficult to persist in working toward them. Here are some strategies for success:

- **Prioritize your goals.** Work toward achieving those that are most important to you. If you have more than one goal, you may not have the energy or resources to achieve them all during the time you specified.

- **Write down your goals.** Having written goals greatly increases your chance of achieving them. Simply thinking about them isn't enough! You must invest the thought and effort to write them down and identify what you need to do to achieve them.

- **Create both immediate and long-term goals.** Make goals for today, next week, next year, and 5 years from now. Ensure that they fit together, so that your short-term goals lead to achieving your long-term goals.

- **Review your goals regularly.** It is critical to regularly review your goals to assess your progress and ensure that you are on the right track. A weekly review is good, but for the best results, a daily review is better. Determine how you are progressing toward your long- and short-term goals. If your short-term goal is to make an 'A' on a test, you should be reviewing your progress daily. This will enable you to evaluate your plan and, if necessary, revise it and get assistance.

- **Avoid procrastination.** Procrastination is one of the biggest challenges you'll face when working toward your goals. Procrastination includes putting things off, making excuses for not doing something, and flat-out laziness. Instead of telling yourself, "I'll do it later," just go ahead and get it done! (You'll find more information on how to beat procrastination in a later chapter.)

- **Don't let others keep you from achieving your goals.**

- **Plan for setbacks.** Setbacks happen, so be prepared. Identify the reason for the setback, the results, and your options for getting back on track. Be **flexible!**

- **Maintain a positive attitude.** Believe in yourself and you can succeed! Each and every time you fall short of a goal, learn from your mistakes and try not to make them again. Remember, none of us is perfect.

- **Keep your goals where you will see them each day.** Seeing your goals on a regular basis will keep them on the forefront of your mind. Post them on your bathroom mirror, calendar, refrigerator, or anywhere that you will see them constantly.

- **Reward yourself when you achieve your goals.** Reward yourself when you reach significant interim goals and major, long-term goals. Rewards can come in many forms. Choose something that is meaningful to you, such as a meal in a restaurant, an extra trip to the gym, a book, or something new to wear.

- **Visualize achieving your goal.** Keep your motivation high by visualizing yourself meeting your goal. Think about the feeling of accomplishment you'll have earned and what that success will mean to you.

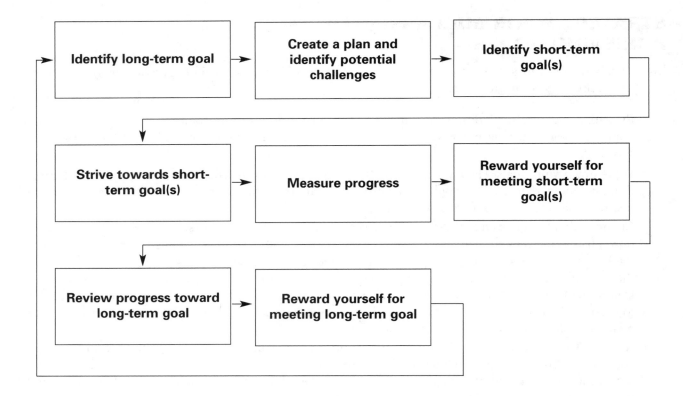

NAME: _____ **DATE:** _____

GOAL SETTING

1. By the end of one week I plan to:
    (Career goal)

    _____
    _____
    _____

    (Academic goal)

    _____
    _____
    _____

    (Personal goal)

    _____
    _____
    _____

    (Social goal)

    _____
    _____
    _____

2. By the end of the term I plan to:
    (Career goal)

    _____
    _____
    _____

    (Academic goal)

    _____
    _____
    _____

    (Personal goal)

    _____
    _____
    _____

    (Social goal)

    _____
    _____
    _____

3. Two years from now I plan to:
   (Career goal)

   _____

   _____

   _____

   (Academic goal)

   _____

   _____

   _____

   (Personal goal)

   _____

   _____

   _____

   (Social goal)

   _____

   _____

   _____

4. Five years from now I plan to:
   (Career goal)

   _____

   _____

   _____

   (Academic goal)

   _____

   _____

   (Personal goal)

   _____

   _____

   (Social goal)

   _____

   _____

   _____

Chapter 5

"What's Your Major?"

LEARNING OBJECTIVES

By the end of this chapter, you should be able to:

Identify your personality type

Explain how to choose a major

Identify the requirements for your TCC degree

Calculate your GPA

CHOOSING A MAJOR

Choosing a major subject to study in college is a huge decision. Many students get the idea that they'll be pursuing their majors for the rest of their lives, but nothing could be further from the truth. Your major should reflect your interests, but it does NOT limit your future goals or plans!

The first step in choosing a major is to identify your interests and strengths. This will help you find the area on which to focus. Remember: your goal is to enjoy your studies, excel at them, and believe in the value of your chosen profession. Consider the subjects you're studying. Which ones interest you? While evaluating your strengths and interests, ask yourself: Would I rather solve problems or write essays? Do I enjoy working in groups or on my own? Am I good at research or would I rather work with my hands?

To clarify your thoughts about choosing a major, complete this simple chart:

Strengths	*Interests*
1.	1.
2.	2.
3.	3.
4.	4.
5.	5.

While evaluating your own strengths and interests will help you choose a major, other assessments help, too.

ASSESSMENTS

Go to the Career Center and complete the "Please Understand Me" assessment, or visit http://www.humanmetrics.com and click on "Jung Typology Test." This test is free. The Self Directed Search, which is a required component of this class, and is provided by your instructor, will be taken during your discussion on careers.. When you have finished the tests, answer the questions below:

Please Understand Me or Myers Briggs Type (Jung Typology Test)

What type are you?

(Circle)

EXTROVERT	INTROVERT
SENSING	INTUITION
THINKING	FEELING
JUDGING	PERCEIVING

Briefly describe your type:

_____

MAKING A MAJOR DECISION

Five Steps

    A.   Don't stress
    B.   Get to know yourself better
    C.   Research and explore your options
    D.   Network
    E.   Don't stress

Questions to ask yourself:

- Which college or university offers your program?
- Where are the departmental offices located?
- Does the required course work for this major compliment your interests and abilities?
- What are the minimum GPA and other prerequisites for this major?
- What courses would it be best to complete while at TCC?
- When is the best time to apply for admission to institutions with this major?
- Is there a required course that may be particularly difficult for you?
- What will the exams in the required courses be like?
- How much freedom will you have to take elective courses?
- What entry-level positions can this degree prepare you for?
- How can you adapt this major to your career objectives?

Your Plan

Here's where the planning starts. You're now a TCC student, and these are the questions to ask yourself:

- What are my goals?
- What degree do I want to earn?
- Where do I want to go from TCC?

TCC offers many options for its students. You can earn an Associate of Arts degree (A.A.), Associate of Science or Associate of Applied Science degrees (A.S. and A.A.S.), or a certificate in any number of occupations.

The A.A degree is designed for students who plan to transfer to a Florida public university as juniors to complete a Bachelor's degree. While at TCC, students take the same courses they would as freshmen and sophomores at a 4-year institution.

For a smooth transition to a public university, TCC students develop an academic plan, called the "*My Success Plan,*" which must include a major and its university prerequisites. Your plan can be accessed through EagleNet, on or off campus or through the TCC Passport, and will need to be completed before meeting with your advisor and/or registering for classes.

Academic advising is crucial to student success, and at Tallahassee Community College, we take it very seriously. Advisors help students choose appropriate classes based on their degree programs and career aspirations. Even when students have already developed their plans, we encourage them to work with an advisor throughout their TCC careers.

The A.A. degree requirements include completing 60 credit hours with satisfactory grades in the following areas:

- Communications (6)
- Humanities (6)
- Mathematics (6)
- Natural science (6)
- Social science (12)
- Electives (24)

Please note that elective hours are best used for university transfer program courses.

The CLAST (College Level Academics Skills Test) is a standardized test that all students in a Florida community college or university must either pass or exempt before receiving an A.A. degree or being admitted to upper division status at a 4-year institution.

It's vital that you choose the right courses if you plan to pursue a particular major at a 4-year institution. Our counselors and faculty advisors will help you acquire the credits to satisfy admissions requirements at universities where you plan to apply. Major-specific course requirements and admissions requirements for individual programs can be found on each school's website.

The most commonly requested websites are listed below:

Florida A&M University, Tallahassee, FL	www.famu.edu
Florida Atlantic University, Boca Raton, FL	www.fau.edu
Florida Gulf Coast University, Ft. Myers, FL	www.fgcu.edu
Florida International University, Miami, FL	www.fiu.edu
Florida State University, Tallahassee, FL	www.fsu.edu
New College of Florida, Sarasota, FL	www.ncf.edu
University of Central Florida, Orlando, FL	www.ucf.edu
University of Florida, Gainesville, FL	www.ufl.edu
University of North Florida, Jacksonville, FL	www.unf.edu
University of South Florida, Tampa, FL	www.usf.edu
University of West Florida, Pensacola, FL	www.uwf.edu

In addition to the university sites, you might find http://FACTS.org useful when you're looking to transfer to a 4-year institution.

If you earn an A.A. degree at TCC, you are guaranteed transfer into the State University System. However, you are not guaranteed transfer into a particular program. The admissions requirements for limited-access programs are more selective and may include a higher GPA, higher test scores, auditions, and/or portfolios. Community college A.A. graduates have the same opportunity to enroll in these programs as students who began their academic careers at that university.

Online transfer manuals can be found in your advising pages. In particular, Florida State University's website on academic majors, http://www.academic-guide.fsu.edu, is extremely

ASSOCIATE IN ARTS DEGREE PLANNING GUIDE

36 hours of General Education:

1. Communications – 6 semester hours

A. ____ ENC 1101 and (3) hours from:

B. ____ ENC 1102
   ____ ENC 1141
   ____ MMC 1100

Communications courses are prerequisites for

2. Humanities – 6 semester hours –

A. ____ HUM 2210 and ____ HUM 2230

OR

B. ____ HUM 2740 and ____ HUM 2741

OR

C. Six (6) hours from two of the following categories:

Art History
____ ARH 2050   ____ ARH 2500Y
____ ARH 2051

Literature
____ AML 2600Y   ____ LIT 2100X
____ AML 2301   ____ THE 2100
____ ENL 2000

Music
____ HUM 2525Y   ____ MUH 2011
____ HUM 2529   ____ MUH 2120X

Philosophy and Religion
____ PHI 2010   ____ REL 2200
____ PHI 2100   ____ REL 2300X
____ PHI 2600

3. Mathematics – 6 semester hours
____ MAC 1105   ____ MAC 2313
____ MAC 2114   ____ MAP 2302
____ MAC 2140   ____ MGF 1106
____ MAC 2233   ____ MGF 1107
____ MAC 2311   ____ STA 2023
____ MAC 2312   ____ STA 2122

4. Sciences – 6 semester hours total from two different categories of science.

A. Biological Science
____ BOT 1000   ____ BSC 1050
____ BSC 1005   ____ BSC 2010
____ BSC 1020   ____ MCB 2004

B. Earth Science
____ ESC 1000   ____ GLY 2160
____ GLY 1030   ____ MET 1010
____ GLY2010   ____ OCE 1001

C. Physical Science
____ AST 1002   ____ PHY 1020
____ CHM 1020   ____ PHY 1053
____ CHM 1030   ____ PHY 2048
____ CHM 1045   ____ PSC 1121

5. History and Social Sciences – 12 semester hours from the following categories.

A. History – 6 hours from options 1, 2, 3,4, 5, or 6
1) ____ AMH 1041 and ____ AMH 1050
2) ____ AMH 2010 and ____ AMH 2020
3) ____ EUH 1000 and ____ EUH 1001
4) ____ WOH 1012 and ____ WOH 1022
5) ____ EUH 1000 and ____ WOH 1022
6) ____ WOH 1012 and ____ EUH 1001

B. Social Sciences – 3 hours
____ ANT 2140
____ ANT 2211X   ____ POS 1041
____ ANT 2410X   ____ POS 1112
____ ANT 2511X   ____ POS 2001
____ CHD 2220   ____ PSY2012
____ CHD 2240   ____ SOP2002
____ CPO 2001   ____ SOP2740Y
____ DEP 2004   ____ SYG 1000
____ ECO 2013   ____ SYG 2010Y
____ ECO 2023   ____ SYG 2230Y
____ GEA 2000X   ____ SYG 2340
____ GEO 1400X   ____ SYG 2361
____ INR 2002   ____ SYG 2430

C. Personal Development – 3 hours from:
____ CLP 1001   ____ HSC 1100
____ HSC 2200

A. Elective Courses – 24 semester hours. Electives are courses which are not being used to satisfy the 36 hours of general education. Use FACTS.org to produce a 2+2 Transfer Evaluation to identify completed prerequisite courses for your major and those that may be taken as electives. Courses completed to satisfy categories B, and C below and *foreign language for university admissions requirements could also be part of the 24 hours of electives required.

B. Instruction in the US Constitution – one course from the following:
____ CPO 2001   ____ POS 1601
____ POS 1041   ____ POS 2001
____ POS 1112

C. Computer Proficiency Requirement:
____ Completed TCC Course with "CC" Designator
____ Completed approved high school course
____ Achieved passing score on TCC exemption exam

D. CLAST
____ Passed all subtests of CLAST
____ CLAST Exempt based on SAT/ACT scores
____ CLAST Exempt based on English & Math GPA

E. A minimum 2.00 TCC GPA and a minimum 2.00 Overall GPA.

X/Y= TCC courses that satisfy FSU's Multicultural Requirement. Also: AMH 2091Y, IDS 2900Y, and LIT 2380Y.

*Note: Florida state universities require two credits of high school sequential foreign language or 8-12 hours at the college-level for admission.

ASSOCIATE IN ARTS DEGREE PLANNING GUIDE

COMMUNICATIONS
ENC 1101, College Composition
ENC 1102, Argument and Persuasion
ENC 1141, Writing About Literature
MMC 1100, Writing for Mass Communication

HUMANITIES
AML 2600, Intro to African American Literature
AML 2301, Major American Writers
ARH 2050, Intro to Art History and Art Criticism I
ARH 2051, Intro to Art History and Art Criticism II
ARH 2500, Non-Western Art History
ENL 2000, British Literature
HUM 2210 & HUM 2230, Humanities of the World I & II
HUM 2740 & HUM 2741, Humanities Abroad I & II
HUM 2525, The American Music Tradition: Jazz
HUM 2529, The American Music Tradition: Popular Music
LIT 2100, Masterpieces of World Literature
MUH 2011, Intro to Music History
MUH 2120, Music of the World
PHI 2010, Philosophy
PHI 2100, Introductory Logic
PHI 2600, Ethics
REL 2200, Intro to Biblical Studies
REL 2300, Intro to World Religions
THE 2100, Intro to Theatre History

SCIENCE
Biological:
BOT 1000, Plant Science
BSC 1020, Intro to Human Biological Sciences
BSC 1050, Environmental Systems
BSC 1005, Intro to the Biological Sciences
BSC 2010, Biology for Science Majors I
MCB 2004, Microbiology
Earth:
ESC 1000, Earth and its Environment
GLY 1030, Environmental Geology
GLY 2010, Physical Geology
GLY 2160, Geology of the National Parks
MET 1010, Meteorology
OCE 1001, Introductory Oceanography

Updated 2/2009

Physical:
AST 1002, Intro to Astronomy
CHM 1020, Chemistry for General Education
CHM 1030, General Chemistry for Allied Health
CHM 1045, General Chemistry I
PHY 1020, Energy and Its Environmental Effects
PHY 1053, Elementary College Physics I
PHY 2048, General Physics I
PSC 1121, Intro to the Physical Sciences

MATHEMATICS
MAC 1105, College Algebra
MAC 2114, Trigonometry
MAC 2140, Precalculus Mathematics
MAC 2311, Calculus with Analytic Geometry I
MAC 2312, Calculus with Analytic Geometry II
MAC 2313, Calculus with Analytic Geometry III
MAC 2233, Calculus for Management and the Non Physical Sciences
MAP 2302, Differential Equation I
MGF 1106, Mathematics I for Liberal Arts
MGF 1107, Mathematics II for Liberal Arts
STA 2023, Intro Statistics I
STA 2122, Intro to Applied Statistics

SOCIAL SCIENCE
Category A, History
AMH 1041 & AMH 1050, American Experience I & II
AMH 2010 & AMH 2020, US. History (Colonial to 1865) & US History (1865 to Present)
EUH 1000 & EUH 1001, History of Western Civilization I & II
WOH 1012 & WOH 1022, History of Civilization I & II

Category B, Social Science
ANT 2140, Introduction to Archaeology
ANT 2211, Peoples of the World
ANT 2410, Introduction to Cultural Anthropology
ANT 2511, Introduction to Physical Anthropology

CHD 2220, Child Development
CHD 2240, Adolescent Development
CPO 2001, Introduction to Comparative Politics
DEP 2004, Human Development
ECO 2013, Principles of Economics (Macro)
ECO 2023, Principles of Economics (Micro)
GEA 2000, World Regional Geography
GEO 1400, Introduction to Human Geography
INR 2002, International Relations
POS 2001, Introduction to Political Science
POS 1041, National Government
POS 1112, State and Local Government
PSY 2012, General Psychology
SOP 2002, Social Psychology
SOP 2740, Psychology of Women
SYG 1000, Principles of Sociology
SYG 2010, Contemporary Social Problems
SYG 2230, Race and Minority Group Relations
SYG 2340, Human Sexuality
SYG 2361, Thanatology: Dying and Death
SYG 2430, Marriage and Family

Category C Personal Development
CLP 1001, Psychology of Personal and Social Adjustment
HSC 1100, Concepts of Positive Living
HSC 2200, Principles of Contemporary Health

ADDITIONAL REQUIREMENTS FOR THE A.A. DEGREE:
INSTRUCTION IN THE U.S. CONSTITUTION
CPO 2001, Intro to Comparative Politics
POS 1601, Foundations of the U. S. Constitution
POS 1041, National Government
POS 1112, State and Local Government
POS 2001, Intro to Political Science

COMPUTER PROFICIENCY SELECTION
See the Tallahassee Community College Catalog for further information.

useful. Approximately 80% of TCC graduates go on to FSU. The College also partners with Flagler College, Embry-Riddle Aeronautical University, Barry University, and St. Leo University, which offer 4-year degrees on TCC's campus. In fact, our University Partners have degree programs in a wide variety of disciplines. TCC's University Partners are housed in the University Center Building on the main campus.

Students enrolled in courses offered by University Partners may access all services available to TCC students. Please call or visit the University Center Building to see which program is right for you.

Barry University at TCC	(850) 385-2279
Embry-Riddle Aeronautical University at TCC	(850) 201-8330
Flagler College at TCC	(850) 201-8070
St. Leo University at TCC	(850) 201-8655

For students who don't plan to transfer to a 4-year institution, TCC offers Associate of Science and Associate of Applied Science degrees (A.S. or A.A.S.). These are 2-year programs that allow you to get credentialed in a high-demand occupation with specific training followed by transition into the workforce.

Please see the TCC catalog for specific A.S. or A.A.S. degree requirements.

If you're not interested in an Associate's degree, TCC offers many occupational certificates. These are short-term programs that boost your skills and offer a means of increasing your income or getting a promotion.

Grade Point Average

The certificate programs at TCC can be completed in one year or less. Whichever degree you choose to seek, one thing is sure, you will need to maintain your GPA in order to better position yourself for whatever the next challenge is. We have included a GPA calculator for you to use not only during this class but for your entire TCC career. You can find GPA calculators online at sites like www.back2 college.com/gpa.htm or by using the calculator on the next page.

SUMMARY

Choosing a major is one of the most important steps to your college career. Some students are so afraid of making a mistake that they procrastinate about it and then have to take extra classes to make up for basics they may have missed along the way. While your choice may change during school, or even after, having a plan in place and a guide to follow will make your college experience much more meaningful. Using the tools provided here will put you on the right path.

COMPUTING YOUR GPA

Points are assigned for each grade that you earn as follows:

Grades	A	B	C	D	F
Points per Credit hour	4	3	2	1	0

To compute (or predict) your semester GPA: List your grades for each course and the number of credit hours in the table below. Then multiply the credit hours for each course by the points from the table above. Add the columns to find H and P.

Example:

Grades	Credit hrs	(pts from above)
B	3	9
C	3	6
D	3	3
F	3	0
TOTAL	12	18
	$18 \div 12 = 1.50$ gpa	

Grades	Credit hrs	(pts from above)
TOTAL	h=	p=

Your semester GPA = (p divided by h) = _____

To compute (or predict) your overall GPA

If you are repeating a course in which you earned the grade of D, you must subtract the grade points earned for that course and the credit hours from the total.

If you are repeating a course in which you earned the grade of F, you will have no points to subtract but you must subtract the number of credit hours from the total.

From your transcript, get the total hours and points that you have earned.

Total hrs credit		Total points from Cum GPA	
Current semester hrs credit		Points from current semester	
TOTAL HRS (H=)		TOTAL PTS (P=)	

GPA = (P divided by H) = _____

Chapter 6

Mastering the Clock: Time Management

YOU SHOULD KNOW

By the end of this chapter you should know:

Where time goes
The connection between setting goals and time management
What procrastination is and how to avoid it

WHERE DOES TIME GO?

Attending college is exhilarating and daunting for most students. From going to class to studying to simply finding your way around campus, the scheduling experience can be a challenge. Add work, family, fitness, and even a social life—and your schedule can run away with you if you don't master it.

That's why time management is so essential. Most students arrive at TCC thinking they can transition as easily from high school to college as they did from elementary to middle school. Not so! Consider: in high school, your schedule was set by others. In the adult realm of college, however, time management begins and ends with as simple a matter as how you handle the first day of class.

Time management is the foundation of college success, and the habits you form now will have a profound effect on whether or not you succeed in the workplace. Many students work full- or part-time, and some are balancing family with school and full employment. Everyone faces their own challenges. In every case, though, their success at time management affects every aspect of their lives.

PERSONAL TIME SURVEY

To begin managing your time you first need a clear idea of how you now use your time. The Personal Time Survey will help you to estimate how much time you currently spend in typical activities. To get a more accurate estimate, you might keep track of how you spend your time for a week. This will help you get a better idea of how much time you need to prepare for each subject. It will also help you identify your time wasters. But for now complete the Personal Time Survey to get an estimate. The following survey shows the amount of time you spend on various activities. When taking the survey, estimate the amount of time spent on each item. Once you have this amount, multiply it by seven. This will give you the total time spent on the activity in 1 week. After each item's weekly time has been calculated, add all these times for the grand total. Subtract this from 168, the total possible hours per week.

HERE WE GO:

1. Number of hours of sleep each night   _____ × 7 = _____

2. Number of grooming hours per day   _____ × 7 = _____

3. Number of hours for meals/snacks per day—
include preparation time   _____ × 7 = _____

4a. Total travel time weekdays   _____ × 5 = _____

4b. Total travel time weekends   _____

5. Number of hours per week for regularly scheduled
functions (clubs, church, get-togethers, etc.)   _____

6. Number of hours per day for chores, errands, extra
grooming, etc.   _____ × 7 = _____

7. Number of hours of work per week   _____

8. Number of hours in class per week   _____

9. Number of average hours per week socializing, dates,
etc. Be honest!   _____

Now add up the totals: _____

Subtract the above number from 168   168 – _____ = _____

The remaining hours are the hours you have allowed yourself to study.

By George Mason University

SETTING GOALS AND TIME MANAGEMENT

Before you devote time to any activity, you should think about how it fits into your life and whether it helps you accomplish any of your goals. If you don't know what your goals are, now is the time to give thoughtful consideration to what you want to do with your life. In his book, *The Seven Habits of Highly Effective People*, Dr. Stephen Covey discusses finding your purpose in life and writing out a personal mission statement. Knowing what you want from your life will help you evaluate how you invest your time. Once you have decided what's important, it's time to set some goals. Note that goals need to be specific, realistic, within your control, and measurable. By setting goals, and systematically working toward achieving them, you will find that your life will have more purpose and meaning. You will accomplish more. We all have the same number of hours each day. The difference between people who are productive and those who seem to drift along—not getting much done is the way they view and use those hours. So how will you manage your time?

To begin managing your time, consider:

- Do you arrange your school schedule around your social life?
- Do you plan vacations or activities that conflict with your studies?
- Do you find yourself saying, "Darn, I didn't get anything done today"?

If you answered yes to one or more of the above questions, then you have a problem with time management. The good news is that you're not alone. You can learn; most adults do. They can balance their activities and meet their obligations in a timely fashion.

- Life is about being prepared for the unexpected. It will turn up sooner or later.
- Minimize the risk of failure by completing tasks ahead of time. That way, when something does go wrong, you'll still be within the margin of error.
- Don't make the mistake of thinking you've got to be in the mood to study. Many students put comfort or pleasure first, as in:
  - "I don't feel like writing my paper now. I'll do it tomorrow."
  - "I'm too tired to study. This weekend, I'll have more energy."
  - "I'll study for my exam when 'American Idol' is over."

The assumption behind these statements is that the person will follow through tomorrow or another day. But the reality for many people is that they procrastinate until their backs are to the wall. Then they don't have enough time to do their best work.

You must challenge yourself to study when you don't feel like it. Make a written schedule and reward yourself when you finish something ahead of time. For instance, don't watch your favorite TV show until you've read 20 pages or completed your math homework. Always remember why you're in college! Academic success requires effective time management to help you achieve your long-term goals.

To determine how many hours you need to study each week to get As, use the following rule of thumb. Study 2 hours per hour in class for an easy class, 3 hours per hour in class for an average class, and 4 hours per hour in class for a difficult class. For example, basket weaving 101 is a relatively easy 3-hour course. Usually, a person would not do more than 6 hours of work outside of class per week for that particular class. Advanced calculus is usually considered a difficult course, so it might be best to study the proposed 12 hours a week. If more hours are needed, take away some hours from easier courses, i.e., basket weaving.

STUDY HOUR FORMULA

Figure out the time that you need to study by using the formula below for each of your classes.

Easy class credit hours   _____ × 2 = _____

Average class credit hours   _____ × 3 = _____

Difficult class credit hours   _____ × 4 = _____

Total   _____

Compare this number to your time left from the survey. Now is the time when many students might find themselves a bit stressed. Just a note to ease your anxieties: it is not only the quantity of study time but also its quality. This formula is a general guideline. Try it for a week, and make adjustments as needed.

CONSIDER THE FOLLOWING SCENARIO

You receive a notice about registering for classes for the upcoming semester. In order to register, you must attend a workshop, set up an appointment with an advisor, select your classes, and pay for your fees. This all must be completed by the end of the month. To add to the challenge, you work part-time and you have a full-time load at school.

What is your plan to successfully complete the following task? Do you have a plan? By not having a plan, how will it cost you?

- Time
- Money
- Opportunity

Time management is about being organized and accountable. That is why time management is so important for college students. As a college student, you're a consumer whose time is a valuable commodity. Analyze your time in terms of dollars and cents—*literally*—and you'll be amazed how much you waste or gain. The choice is yours to make.

WHY IS TIME MANAGEMENT SO IMPORTANT?

You might have heard these sayings "Fail to plan, plan to fail," or, "Time is money." Nothing could be truer for the college student. Using our time wisely is as important as using our money wisely. When it's gone, you can't get it back.

Unlike high school where your classes and extracurricular activities are established for you, once you enter college YOU are in charge of scheduling your activities, whether it's classes, hours to work, or extracurricular activities. Managing your time successfully in those areas is the first key in making your college experiences a huge success. While it can be very intimidating, if you do not establish proper time management techniques, it will **cost** you.

WHAT ARE THE KEYS TO SUCCESSFULLY MANAGING YOUR TIME AS A COLLEGE STUDENT?

Beating Procrastination

When it comes to time management for a student, it's Public Enemy Number One. Procrastination is defined as habitually delaying or postponing activities. It's a prevailing issue for most of us and poses a serious problem for college students who can't recognize and overcome it.

Procrastination manifests itself in many ways and can become very debilitating for a student who does not properly use time management strategies. So how do you combat procrastination?

The following is a Seven Day Anti-Procrastination strategy that if used, and used properly, will provide an opportunity to stop the cycle of procrastination:

Monday: Make it meaningful. What is important about the job you've been putting off? List all the benefits of completing it. Look at it in relation to your goals. Be specific about the rewards for getting it done including how you will feel when the task is complete.

Tuesday: Take it apart. Break the big jobs into a series of small ones you can do in 15 minutes or less. If a long reading assignment intimidates you, divide it into two-page or three-page sections. Make a list of the sections and cross them off as you complete them so you can see your progress.

Wednesday: Write an Intention Statement on a 3 × 5 card. For example, if you can't get started on a term paper, you might write, "I intend to write a list of at least 10 possible topics by 9 p.m. I will reward myself with an hour of guilt-free recreational reading." Carry the 3 × 5 card with you or post it in your study area where you can see it often.

Thursday: Tell everyone, announce publicly, your intention to get it done. Tell a friend you intend to learn 10 irregular French verbs by Saturday. Tell your spouse, roommate, parents, and children. Include anyone who will ask whether you've completed it or who will suggest ways to get it done. Make the world your support group.

Friday: Find a reward. Construct rewards carefully. Be willing to withhold them if you do not complete the task. Don't pick a movie as a reward for studying biology if you plan to go to the movie anyway. And when you legitimately reap your reward, notice how it feels.

Saturday: Settle it now. Do it now. The minute you notice yourself procrastinating, plunge into the task. Imagine yourself at a mountain lake, poised to dive. Gradual immersion would be slow torture. It's often less painful to leap. Then be sure to savor the feeling of having the task behind you.

Sunday: Say no. When you keep pushing a task into the low-priority category, reexamine the purpose for doing it at all. If you realize you really don't intend to do something, quit telling yourself that you will. That's procrastinating. Just say NO! Then you're not procrastinating, and you don't have to carry around the baggage of an undone task.

In some cases, procrastination is positive. Consider the following possibilities:

1. Procrastinate deliberately. You might discover that if you choose to procrastinate, you can also choose not to procrastinate.

2. Observe your procrastination. Instead of doing something about it, look carefully at the process and its consequences. Avoid judgments. Be a scientist and record the facts. See if procrastination keeps you from getting what you want. Seeing clearly the cost of procrastination may help you kick the habit.

3. Ask yourself whether it's a problem. As one writer put it, "I don't do my best work because of a tight deadline. I do my only work with a tight timeline." Some people thrive under pressure and maybe that style works for you.

Remember: you can do it. By developing your skills and a positive attitude, you will succeed.

KEYS TO TIME MANAGEMENT SUCCESS

Getting Organized

First, get a copy of the *TCC Student Handbook and Planner,* which includes a calendar with important dates (registration, exam week, etc.) and plenty of room to note daily tasks. It also includes key campus resources and logistics. Stop by the Office of Campus Life on the first floor of the Student Union for your planner. Keep it with you; you'll be able to jot down assignments and exams as they're announced. You'll also be able to size up your week at a glance, planning for tests, study sessions, meetings with professors, and social events. This will enable you to merge your on- and off-campus priorities.

It's best to use the planner from the beginning of the school term. By the third day of class, each instructor will have given you a syllabus and, once you've received yours, start putting test dates, review dates, term paper, and project due dates into your planner. While always subject to change, this is the blueprint of your semester.

If you work full- or part-time, include your work hours. If you're employed part-time, then your class attendance and study time must come before work. If you have a full-time job, however, schedule classes that won't conflict with work and be realistic about how many credit hours you can handle. Many students register for courses only to drop them midway through the semester due to work constraints.

Keep a folder for each class and reorganize them throughout the year. Start now. Remember: review your planner at the beginning of every week, also noting the week ahead. This ensures that you don't encounter conflicts in your schedule. It's also important because professors don't always give advance notice on a quiz or homework assignment.

Successful time management means taking responsibility for your own priorities.

Taking Care of Yourself

Many students don't realize it, but your sleep patterns and how you schedule classes are very important. There's a big difference between morning larks and night owls! Morning people wake up early, ready to tackle the day. Night owls are most alert and active in the evening; they struggle to get to an early morning class. Generally, young adults are night owls. If you're one, take night classes or, if you must take a morning class, discipline yourself to go to bed earlier.

Many college students take nutrition for granted. It's trite but true that breakfast is the most important meal of the day, providing energy and coherence. If you attend an early morning class without eating first, most likely you won't hear the lecture over the growling of your stomach. In a perfect world, a leisurely, well-balanced breakfast would keep us attentive in class, but a protein bar or yogurt will do just fine.

Having Realistic Expectations

If you coasted through high school with a C average, you'll find that at TCC, as at any institution of higher learning, you must raise your standards. The pace in college is much faster and your instructors' expectations are higher than in high school. Instructors rarely tolerate students who show up late for class, and they won't repeat part of a lecture if you daydream and miss it.

Unfortunately, many students believe that if a class doesn't work out this time around, they can retake it later. What a waste of time, effort, and money! Instead, talk with your advisor prior to scheduling your classes to make sure that they're right for you. Talk with your professors before registering or during the first week of class; this will give you a realistic sense of how you'll perform.

Avoiding Over-Committing

This is where students struggle most with time management. For instance, those who were high achievers in high school get to college and, naturally, want to continue their involvement in student government, sororities or fraternities, clubs, or intramural sports. In some cases, in fact, extracurricular activities are students' main reason for attending college; they may miss lots of classes or, worse, fail a course rather than give up a nonacademic activity. It's tempting to get involved in low-priority activities, such as a club meeting, because they're fun, whereas high-priority activities like studying for a test are associated with anxiety.

You must recognize the primary reason you're in college. To receive a well-rounded educational experience, recognize your boundaries. It doesn't help your collegiate experience to be president of every club on campus if you're also on academic probation.

Getting Real about School

Many students come to college believing every day is a holiday. They expect all instructors to be engaging and witty. They want everyone they meet to plan a party every Saturday night. In reality, however, college is highly competitive. Stay focused and motivated. Your college experience depends on your self-discipline and successful interaction with others, which is based to a great extent on meeting your deadlines. Learn to communicate with your instructors and other TCC staffers, such as librarians and tutors, who are here to assist you.

SUMMARY

To recap, here is a little checklist of time management to-do's:

- Use your Planner (i.e., Your TCC Planner)
- Recognize how much time you need to spend on class work, activities, work, etc.
- Recognize how much time you have to do certain things. What do you do in 24 hours?
- Is your "free time" really free?
  - Use free time to catch up on class work
  - Look ahead to see what reading assignments/homework is due at the end of the week
- Recognize your daily college schedule is different than your daily high school schedule
- Leave time during the day for yourself
- Weekends—don't let them get away from you (6:00 p.m. on a Sunday night is not a good time to start your homework)
- Make a list of To-Dos (daily, weekly, or both)
- Be Flexible—don't fall apart if you don't get everything done or your schedule changes
- Set weekly goals and reward yourself when you reach them
- Use an alarm clock

The techniques in this chapter are useful tools for successful time management. However, they can enable you to succeed only if you practice them on a consistent, regular basis. They can boost your success in school, work, and life immensely. Remember: learn from the mistakes you make as a result of poor time management, and you'll learn to find time for what matters to you.

"Time is life. It is irreversible and irreplaceable. To waste time is to waste your life, but to control time is to master your life and make the most of it."

— ALAN LAKEIN, WORLD EXPERT ON PERSONAL TIME MANAGEMENT

NAME: _____ **DATE:** _____

ACTIVITY

Using your current schedule and your semester calendar, make up a weekly schedule for next week using the chart below. Be sure to indicate your classes, work hours, and study times along with your regular activities. Be as detailed as possible.

Time	Monday	Tuesday	Wednesday	Thursday	Friday	Saturday	Sunday
12:00 AM							
12:30 AM							
1:00 AM							
1:30 AM							
2:00 AM							
2:30 AM							
3:00 AM							
3:30 AM							
4:00 AM							
4:30 AM							
5:00 AM							
5:30 AM							
6:00 AM							
6:30 AM							
7:00 AM							
7:30 AM							
8:00 AM							
8:30 AM							
9:00 AM							
9:30 AM							
10:00 AM							
10:30 AM							
11:00 AM							
11:30 AM							
12:00 PM							
12:30 PM							
1:00 PM							
1:30 PM							
2:00 PM							
2:30 PM							
3:00 PM							
3:30 PM							
4:00 PM							
4:30 PM							
5:00 PM							
5:30 PM							
6:00 PM							
6:30 PM							
7:00 PM							
7:30 PM							
8:00 PM							
8:30 PM							
9:00 PM							
9:30 PM							
10:00 PM							
10:30 PM							
11:00 PM							
11:30 PM							

Chapter 7

"Show Me the Money"— Money Management

LEARNING OBJECTIVES

By the end of this chapter you should be able to:

Develop a budget

Understand income versus expense

Recognize sound credit card practices

Have a background in sound investing

Sound financial planning will help you in college and in everything else you do. Whether your goal is to complete your A.A. degree, buy a car, or simply have dinner with a friend, how you manage your money has a huge impact on your ability to achieve your goals. Many people live paycheck to paycheck, making minimal or no effort to save. Without money saved, unexpected expenses can cause you great anxiety because they can easily result in debt and a continuing drain on your time and resources.

Learning how to create a budget, spend within your means, and manage your money can be a daunting task, but the information in this chapter should provide you with the basics. Money management skills are necessary to ensure that you are able to pay your bills, stay out of debt, and have the cash to go out on weekends or splurge on a shopping trip. A strong financial plan will help if you encounter unexpected financial problems while in college, as well as laying the groundwork for life goals such as saving for a home. You don't want lack of financial planning to cause you to withdraw from college!

GETTING CONTROL OF YOUR MONEY

Set Personal Spending Goals

You learned in the chapter on goals how to identify and set long- and short-term goals. How much money do these goals require? For goals such as college, buying a car, or improving on your home, it will take substantial saving and planning. Look at your budget and decide if you can save enough money for your goal, whether you'll need financial assistance from a bank, or if you should reevaluate your budget. If you need help financing college, TCC's Financial Aid Department can guide you.

Track Your Money

Many of us don't really know how much we spend on flexible expenses. Let's see how you *actually* spend your money by tracking your expenditures for at least 6–8 weeks. For the next 4 weeks, carry a small pocket notebook or PDA, and enter everything that you purchase every day. This may seem like a lot of work, but it is a proven way to understand how you spend your money! Tracking your purchases will, in turn, help you get control of your spending and change your spending habits.

At the end of the first 4 weeks, add up your flexible expenses and enter the appropriate information in the budget sheet. Have you spent more than you earned? What did you spend your money on? Now, repeat this tracking method for another 2–4 weeks, trying to reduce the amount you spend. Again, review your expenditures. Did you reduce the amount spent on spur-of-the-moment purchases or impulsive entertainment?

Spend within Your Means

You don't want to make a habit of spending more than you earn, since that is how people end up with high credit card or loan balances that they cannot pay down. After filling in the Monthly Budget form, did you have a ***negative cash flow***? A negative cash flow means that your expenses are more than your income. In that case, you'll want to look for ways to cut your costs. Are you spending a lot on clothes? Do you really need that daily cappuccino or bagel? Some easy ways to cut expenses are eating at home, packing snacks, buying clothes on sale, and using public transportation. These types of savings can really make a big difference at the end of the month.

Start Saving

Look at your budget again. Do you have a ***positive cash flow***? A positive cash flow means you spent less than you made. In addition to creating a budget, you'll want to start a saving habit. The amount you save each month doesn't really matter at first. Even saving $5 a week can really add up quickly. The savings can then be used instead of your charge card for emergencies. Put the money in an out-of-the-way place, or better yet, open a savings account. Having at least 2 to 4 months' worth of living expenses in savings would see you through an emergency, such as an illness or job loss. If you have the goal of a new car or a new home, you might want to take another look at your budget and identify additional ways to save. Make sure you don't cut back so far that you aren't able to hold to your budget or enjoy yourself. Remember, the key is to stick to your budget and pay your bills on time.

BORROWING MONEY
Establishing a Good Credit History

Having a good credit history is crucial when trying to obtain a credit card or take out loans for school, a car, a home, or starting a business. In addition, many employers will run a credit check on new and current employees. Why? For some businesses, such as a bank, it's because you might be dealing with money. For others, a strong credit history demonstrates your ability to manage money and meet your commitments. This also shows potential employers that you are a responsible and dependable person, something they look for in employees.

Establishing or repairing credit can be extremely frustrating for a student who doesn't have established credit. The bank won't give you a credit card or a loan, since you don't have a credit history, and you can't build your credit history because you can't get a loan or a credit card. Another potential problem: not being able to obtain credit because you've defaulted on a school loan or not made timely loan payments. Open a free student checking account and a savings account. This helps in establishing your credit score, and also helps you avoid paying large check-cashing fees. You can also set up a direct deposit from your checking account into your savings account. Remember, money unseen is money unspent.

If you don't have a credit history or you have poor credit, start immediately to create a positive credit history. Get your apartment lease, phone, or utilities in your name. You may need to have someone with good credit cosign your lease the first year. After 1 year, check with your landlord, phone, or utility company to determine if you have enough of a credit history to be the sole signature on your account. You might also try to get a gas card or store card in your own name. Remember to limit the number of your credit cards. Having just one or two is best until you are sure you won't get yourself in debt trouble. Students frequently fail to realize how quickly and easily they can get into credit debt. To create a good credit history, pay your bills on time. Paying your bills on time will also help repair a poor credit history.

Your Credit Report

Your credit history is provided in a **credit report** and is recorded as a **credit score**. Your credit report is a detailed list of your credit history. Residents of all states, including Florida, and most other states can get one free credit report from each of the three credit reporting agencies once a year through Annual Credit Report.com (http://www.annualcreditreport.com). For a small fee, you can obtain a copy at any time directly from the credit bureaus:

Equifax: 1-800-685-1111 or http://www.equifax.com

Experian: 1-888-397-3742 or http://www.experian.com

TransUnion: 1-800-916-8800 or http://www.transunion.com

You should review your credit report at least *once a year*. This will enable you to check for errors or fraud. Your credit report covers, but is not limited to:

- Name
- Birth date

MONTHLY INCOME	(EXAMPLE of completed worksheet)	
	Income/salary after taxes	2,0000.
Enter your monthly income	Investment income	0
	Other income (student loans, parents, etc)	800.00
	Total Monthly Income	2,800.00

MONTHLY EXPENSES

Housing		Food			
		Groceries	350.00	**Enter housing and food totals**	
Rent / Mortgage	850.00	Eating out	50.00		
Other		Other	30.00		
Total Housing	850.00	Total Food	430.00	Total Housing	850.00
				Total Food	430.00

Utilities		Car/Transportation			
Laundry(dry cleaning/ laundry mat)	15.00	Public transit	0	**Enter Utilities and Transportation totals**	
Gas/electricity	300.00	Car loan/lease	0		
Water	0	Car insurance	100.00		
Garbage	45.00	Maintenance	0		
Cell Phone/Phone	60.00	Parking	0		
Internet access	0	Gas	75.00		
Other	0	Other	0		
Total Utilities	455.00	Total Car/Transportation	175.00	Total Utilities	455.00
				Total Car/Transportation	175.00

Insurance		Loan/ Credit Balance			
Renters / Homeowners	0		0	**Enter Insurance and Loan/Credit totals**	
Health/Medical	0	Credit Card	0		
Disability	0	Home Equity Loan/Line	0		
Life	0	Personal Loan/Line	0		
Dental	0	Education Loans	0		
Other	0	Other	0		
Total Insurance	0	Total Loan/Outstanding Credit Card Balance	0	Total Insurance	0
				Total Loan/Outstanding Credit Card Balance	0

Personal/Miscellaneous		Entertainment			
Cosmetics/Toiletries	10.00	Movies	20.00	**Enter Personal and Entertainment totals**	
Clothing	50.00	Vacation	0		
Pharmacy	20.00	Parties/Party supplies	50.00		
Gifts	10.00	Other	0		
Other	0	Total Entertainment	70.00	Total Entertainment	70.00
Total Personal/Miscellaneous	90.00			Total Personal/Miscellaneous	90.00

Enter Monthly Income and total from the top of the page	Total Monthly Expenses	2,070.00
	Total Monthly Income	2,800.00
	Subtract Total Monthly Expenses	2,070.00
	Cash Flow	730.00

MONTHLY INCOME (Income per semester if including financial aid must be divided by 4 to get a true picture.)

Income/salary after taxes	
Investment income	
Other income (student loans, parents, etc)	
Total Monthly Income	

MONTHLY EXPENSES

Housing		**Food**	
Rent / Mortgage		Groceries	
Association Dues		Eating out	
Other		Other	
Total Housing		Total Food	

Total Housing	
Total Food	

Utilities		**Car/Transportation**	
Laundry(dry cleaning/ laundra-mat)		Public transit	
Gas/electricity		Car loan/lease	
Water		Car insurance	
Garbage		Maintenance	
Cell Phone/Phone		Parking	
Internet access		Gas	
Other		Other	
Total Utilities		Total Car/Transportation	

Total Utilities	
Total Car/Transportation	

Insurance		**Loan/Credit Balance**	
Renters / Homeowners		Credit Card	
Health/Medical		Home Equity Loan/Line	
Disability		Personal Loan/Line	
Life		Education Loans	
Dental		Other	
Other			
Total Insurance		Total Loan/Outstanding Credit Card Balance	

Total Insurance	
Total Loan/Outstanding Credit Card Balance	

Personal/Miscellaneous		**Entertainment**	
Cosmetics/Toiletries		Movies	
Clothing		Vacation	
Pharmacy		Parties/Party supplies	
Gifts		Other	
Other		Total Entertainment	
Total Personal/Miscellaneous			

Total Entertainment	
Total Personal/Miscellaneous	

	Total Monthly Expenses	
(housing, utilities, insurance, misc)	**Total Monthly Income**	
	Subtract Total Monthly Expenses	
	Cash Flow	

- Employment history
- Account balances
- Type of credit (auto loan, mortgage, etc.)
- Credit limits and loan amounts
- Payment history
- Bankruptcies

This is important to do even if you believe that you have no credit history. Credit fraud and identity theft can happen to anyone, whether they have established credit histories or not.

A *credit score*, sometimes referred to as your credit rating, is a numeric value. This value is based on the information contained in your credit report. You want your credit score to be high, as the score tells a potential lender the risk level they incur that you will not pay, or will make late payments. Remember, loaning money is a business, and banks want to make sure that they will get their money back. As all three agencies use a scale of 300–850 when rating credit it is important to know that the *higher* your score, the *lower* the risk potential for lenders. When applying for a loan, there are many more factors than just your credit score that lenders will use to determine your actual interest rates, but a good credit score always helps.

BORROW WISELY

Borrow only if it is *absolutely* necessary and only for the amount you truly need. Don't take out a loan for $15,000 when all you need is $5,000. Before you borrow for school, check out how much it will cost you to attend TCC for a year. The Financial Aid Department can help. You will want to determine your personal expenses and the cost of attending college. Use the *Budget Sheet* or the software of your choice to create your personal budget. Most important, pay your loans on time. You don't want late payments to damage your credit history. In addition, paying on time will help you avoid expensive late fees. Those late fees add up quickly.

> According to the Center for Economic and Policy Research, using data from the College Board, approximately two-thirds of all students use loans to pay for their higher education. The average debt for students graduating in 2006 (the latest data available) was $21,000 for most students at public schools and $22,581 for private.

Now that you are a college student, many lenders will start to inundate you with credit card offers. You will find such offers in your email, mailbox, textbooks, and at bank representative booths on campus. Do you know why banks want you to use their credit cards? Because they need to establish new borrowers! The interest accrued from your use of a credit card is an important way that banks make money. In addition, college students tend to be impulse buyers of small purchases, such as clothing and fast food, and those expenses can add up quickly. Let's say you spend $10 a day on a cappuccino in the morning and fast food for lunch. That would add up to $200 a month! You can avoid spending more than you can afford by having a budget and keeping control of how you use your credit card.

CREDIT CARDS
Choose the Best Card for You

Once you have decided to get a card, you should first look for the bank offering the lowest fixed percentage rate with a low or no annual fee. Be sure to read the entire document, even the fine print. Many credit cards with low or 0% introductory rate offers expire in 6–12 months and then shoot up to a high interest rate. Some students use cards with frequent-flyer miles or other specialized cards that frequently have a monthly fee or higher interest rate. You should only use credit cards if you know you can pay off the bill each month.

If this is your first card, or you are repairing your credit, you'll want to stick with a card with a low interest rate. Start out with a low credit limit, such as $500 or $1,000. That will normally be enough for any emergency you might encounter, such as a car repair bill or visit to the doctor. Even if you have good credit and have a card with a higher limit, keep a credit card with a lower limit to use when shopping online to help safeguard against fraudulent charges.

PRECAUTIONS FOR PREVENTING FRAUD

- **Your Social Security number should never be given out unless absolutely necessary.**

  Carry only necessary forms of identification and charge cards. If you don't normally use a credit card, such as a store or gas card, don't carry it. Store your marriage license, insurance papers, and other documents that you don't need to use or carry on a regular basis in a securely locked place, such as a safety deposit box. Make electronic copies of important information, such as a driver's license and keep it with your other secured documents. You will then be prepared to provide the information to the police or the bank customer service representatives.

- **Limit the number of statements you send and receive through the mail.** Statements contain personal information (social security number, bank account number), so the fewer sent through the mail, the less chance there is for someone to obtain and use your identity fraudulently.

- **Limit the credit offers you receive in the mail.** You don't want someone filling one of the offers in your name! If you would like to reduce the number of credit offers you receive, contact the National Consumer Credit Reporting Agencies (NCCRA).

- **Shred ALL statements, bills, and documents containing your personal or financial information before you throw them out.** It really *is* true that most fraud and identity thefts happen as a result of "dumpster diving" and mail theft, so be sure to shred all your documents.

- **Regularly review your credit report.** Do this *at least* once a year; look for any inaccuracies and discrepancies.

- **Keep your name off marketing lists.** The Direct Marketing Association (DMA) membership consists of agencies and companies that compile mailing and telemarketing lists. The DMA is responsible for notifying members to remove individual names from their lists.

(continued)

PRECAUTIONS FOR PREVENTING FRAUD (continued)

Email and Your Online Security

- **Don't write your passwords down or share them with others.** Instead you should memorize your passwords. When creating passwords, use combinations of letters and numbers. Most importantly, your Social Security number should never be used as a username or password. Change your passwords regularly.

- **Always be wary of suspicious emails.** Avoid opening any questionable emails, such as those mentioning that information is needed to be awarded a prize. If you accidentally responded with personal information to a suspicious email, call the Online Fraud Prevention hotline at 1-866-867-5568.

- **Check for the latest "phishing" and other email scams.** Phishing emails are made to look as if they come from a reputable bank or other company. They will frequently ask you to verify/update your account information as a reply to the email or by going to the website link provided, where the information can be entered. Most banks maintain and regularly update a list of phishing scams being investigated.

Credit Card and Online Bank Account Security

- **Keep your online banking, ATM, and credit card passwords secure.** As with your email, don't write down your username or passwords. Don't ever use your Social Security number as your username for an online account.

- **Exercise caution when using an ATM.** Be aware of who is around you when using an ATM. Make sure it's safe.

- **Review credit card account statements carefully.** This is one of the easiest ways to catch fraudulent activity quickly, so be sure to check your statements each month! Inform your bank or charge card company about suspicious charges. The contact number is printed on the bank statement.

- **Report lost or stolen credit/debit cards or checks to your bank immediately.** Don't delay! Call your credit company as soon as you realize that a card is missing.

Phone and Mail Precautions

- **Deposit your outgoing mail at a U.S. Postal Service mail box and collect your mail as soon as possible.** Don't want to give anyone an opportunity to retrieve your mail from your mailbox.

- **Know when you should be receiving your monthly bills and bank statement.** Contact the customer service department immediately if you don't receive your normal monthly bill or statement.

- **Never give out personal information over the telephone.**

Tips for Managing Your Credit Card Debt

Tip 1: Take responsibility for your spending. There are very good reasons to obtain and use credit cards. The key is to be a responsible borrower! Credit cards are an excellent way to establish a credit history and are very convenient to use. Credit cards allow you to buy online, over the phone, and/or from catalogs. You can use them for travel, shopping, restaurants, and emergency expenditures. In many cases, such as renting a car, you must have a card; your cash won't do. As you can see, there are many valid uses for credit, but the convenience also gets people in trouble; it's very easy to lose sight of how much you spend!

Credit card companies require a minimum monthly payment on your balance. Consider, if you owe $3,000 on your card with an Annual Percentage Rate (APR) of 12% and the minimum monthly payment is 2.5% of your current balance, it would take you 175 payments to pay off the loan and you would have paid $1,846.73 in interest! Check out a debt repayment calculator such as http://www.bankrate.com and calculate how long it would take you to repay your loan and how much interest you will pay based on your current payments. Remember that using a credit card of any sort is not a free bank service.

Tip 2: Pay bills on time. Using your credit card wisely is part of being a responsible borrower. It is essential that you pay your bills on time to maintain good credit.

Tip 3: Use your card for emergency expenses only and don't go over your credit limit.

Tip 4: Keep track of your credit card spending. You should always know your current credit card debt amount. Save your credit card receipts and regularly check your records with the bank online. This is a free service, so use it frequently! You should also check your statement each month against your receipts to ensure that it is accurate. Contact your card lender immediately if you notice a discrepancy or don't feel you placed a specific charge on your card.

Tip 5: Only use cash advances for absolute emergencies. Cash advances have much higher interest rates and fees, and therefore are the most costly way for you to use credit.

Tip 6: Do not exceed your credit line. Your *available credit* is how much credit you have left on your credit account, while your *credit line* is the total amount you are allowed to borrow. Your *outstanding balance* is the amount that you currently owe in credit card debt. If possible, keep at least a 15–25% cushion of available credit in your account in case of a financial emergency.

Tip 7: Make regular payments. It is best to pay off the entire charge each month, but if you are unable to do so, pay the *total minimum due* plus a little more. Paying more than the total minimum due will help reduce the interest costs. You should at least pay the minimum payment due each month.

Tip 8: Do not skip a monthly payment. Not only will you be hit with late payment fees, nonpayment of your bills will hurt your credit rating! Late payments stay on your credit report for 7 years and bankruptcy stays on your credit report for 10 years.

SAVING VERSUS INVESTING

Saving and investing are terms that are sometimes used interchangeably, but it is very important to know the difference. Both saving and investing have a place in your finances. With savings, your principal typically remains constant and earns interest or dividends. Savings are kept in certificates of deposit (CDs), checking accounts, money market accounts, and passbook savings accounts. In comparison, investments can go up or down in value and may or may not pay interest or dividends. Examples of investments include stocks, bonds, mutual funds, collectibles, precious metals, and real estate.

WHAT DO YOU NEED TO START INVESTING?

You don't need a lot of money to start investing you just need to start! Look over your budget. If you have as little as $50 a month available, you can start investing, but savings can begin with any amount. Just do it.

TWO MYTHS ABOUT INVESTING

Myth 1

You need a lot of money to invest. Not so. For example, most mutual funds require a minimum investment of $2,000 to $3,000. However, some will allow you to open a fund with as little as $50 if you agree to have that amount automatically deposited monthly from your checking account. Mutual funds are not your only option; there are many other investment options where you can participate with a minimal monthly condition.

Myth 2

You'll need to pay a financial advisor to help you invest. A lot of investments can be purchased without consulting a financial advisor. You just need to do some research, which is much like what you do when you are looking to purchase something online as well.

The truth is that investors generally start out small—especially when they're young. The great thing about investing when you're young is that you have the luxury of time—time to watch your tiny investment grow. Be patient, be careful (but not too careful), and have fun.

RECENT GRADUATE	NOT-SO-RECENT GRADUATE
• Begins investing for retirement at age 21	• Begins investing for retirement at age 30
• Invests $2000 each year until 29 and does not invest any more money for retirement after that	• Invests $2000 each year and continues to do so until 65
• Total contributions: $18,000 at a 10% compounded rate of return	• Total contributions: $70,000 at a 10% compounded rate of return
• Value at age 65: $839,556	• Value at age 65: $598,253

INTRODUCTION TO RISK AND RETURN

Before investing your money, you will have to understand the important concept of **risk and return**. Risk and return means that the returns you will get when investing your money will vary. You may even lose money. However, no matter what you do with your money, you are always taking some amount of risk. If you keep your money at home, you risk that it could be lost or stolen. If you place your money in a bank account, you risk that the returns that you get will not be high enough.

Risk and return also means that if you take greater risks, you should expect to get greater returns. If you want the possibility of getting greater returns, you need to invest your money in more risky investments, for example bonds or stocks. Different bonds and stocks even have different degrees of risk. So, how much risk should you take with your money? That depends on many different factors including your age, risk tolerance, and investment objectives. No matter where you invest your money, you first should understand the investment's risks and potential rewards.

The following exercise will help you to begin to look at return and risk.

EXERCISE

You have been given the option to invest in either a safe investment, or one that has more risk. The safe investment will give you a return of 5%. The risky investment's return will vary. Finish filling in the following table, and answer the questions that follow:

SAFE INVESTMENT: Here is the return for the safe investment. It will always give the same return.

Money to Invest	Return	Gain(Loss)	Total
$1,000.00	5%	$50.00	$1,050.00

RISKY INVESTMENT: The risky investment's return will vary and may be one of the following. Finish filling in the following table. Round each calculation to the nearest penny.

	Money to Invest	Return	Gain/Loss	Total
1.	$1,000.00	−8%		$_____
2.	$1,000.00	−2%		$_____
3.	$1,000.00	6%		$_____
4.	$1,000.00	17%		$_____
5.	$1,000.00	1%		$_____
6.	$1,000.00	−6%		$_____

Should you choose the safe investment or the risky investment? Why?

FINDING THE BEST CREDIT CARD

Credit card costs and features can vary greatly. This exercise will give you a chance to shop for and compare the costs and features of three credit cards.

Using the attached form, research the costs and features of:

- Two major credit cards; and
- One credit card from a department store.

When you're done, answer the following questions.

What did you find?

1. Which credit card has the highest annual percentage rate and how much is it?
2. What method is used to calculate the monthly finance charge for the first major credit card?
3. When does the finance charge begin to accrue on the credit card from the local department store?
4. Do any of the cards have annual fees? If so, which one(s) and how much is the fee?
5. Is there a transaction fee on any card? If so, how much is it?
6. Is there a minimum finance charge on either of the major credit cards? If so, how much is it?
7. Does the first major credit card charge a fee for late payments? If so, how much is it?
8. What is the grace period on the credit card from the local department store?
9. Rafael needs to buy new tires for his truck that cost $450. According to his budget, he can afford payments up to $62.00 per month. Which of the three credit cards you've found would you recommend that Rafael use to purchase the tires? Is there a more prudent way for Rafael to get the tires? Explain.

Use the form on the following page to compare the three credit cards:

Using the attached form, research the costs and features of:

	CARD ONE	CARD TWO	CARD THREE
Type of Account: Credit Card Charge Card			
Company name, address, phone			
Website			
Locations where card is accepted			
Annual fee (if any)			
Grace period			
Annual Percentage Rate (APR)			
Finance charge calculation method			
Credit limit			
Minimum payment			
Other fees: Late payment			
Other features			

SUMMARY

Learning to manage your money now, while still in college, may not seem important, but it is a lesson that as you get older you will be glad you learned. Whether you agree with the principle or not, money is what makes the world go around and knowing how to manage yours can make your personal world a much nicer place. Develop a savings plan while you're young and it will pay you back tremendously when you are ready to buy a house or send a child to college. This savings plan can also help during emergencies, those things that happen unexpectedly like your car breaking down or your financial aid being late. Emergencies don't include dinner out with friends or trips to the beach for the weekend.

Develop a budget while you are a struggling student and when you have a job with income to cover your expenses, the principle makes life so much simpler. Take the lessons learned in this chapter and use them. They will make not only your time in college, but your life, sweeter.

For further information on any of the details covered in this chapter and as a resource that will come in handy for you when buying a car, house or making an investment, please check out the following website:

http://www.tcc.fl.edu/about_tcc/student_affairs/student_services/online_financial_resource_center

This website was developed for TCC students by a member of our faculty.

Chapter 8

The Way I Learn

LEARNING OBJECTIVES

By the end of this chapter you should be able to:

Define learning style

Define internal and external stimuli

Identify course delivery formats

List and define the three types of learning styles

Identify personal learning style(s)

Write a summary comparison of the different learning styles

WHAT IS YOUR PREFERRED LEARNING AND STUDY ENVIRONMENT(S)?

Take a moment to think about how and when you prefer to learn, both in and out of class. Can you concentrate better in the morning or at night? Are you an independent learner? Do you like the face-to-face interaction and more structured learning environment of an on-campus course? In college, it is vital to identify your preferred way of learning, which will help you to recall and apply what you've learned more effectively.

Learning and Study Environment

You need at least one place where you feel comfortable studying. If possible, choose a spot that will be your primary study spot: your desk, a library, a coffee shop, or a bookstore. Reading in bed definitely isn't a good idea, because it's too easy to lay your work aside and your head down to nap! In order to form a good study habit, choose one or two areas to study and use them consistently.

Also consider how well you study alone, with a friend, or in a group. Did you know that participating in a study group can increase your motivation and learning? You will be better organized and motivated to learn because your group will be counting on you to do your share. Each member can benefit from a study group, even those who have a stronger understanding of the material. Sharing your knowledge with the group will reinforce, clarify, and deepen your own understanding of the material. If you enjoy studying with others, contact your instructor about the best way to get a study group together. If your course is web-assisted or web-based, your instructor may be able to set up an online area just for your study group. Most libraries have study rooms for students, so inquire about their availability and make a reservation. There will be many opportunities during your college career for you to utilize all types of study environments. Learn to use them to your advantage so that you can succeed.

While you won't always be able to choose the learning environment that your course is delivered in, understanding your learning styles and preferences will help you identify what delivery format best fits your needs. There are a wide variety of formats, including self-paced, web-based, televised, and on-campus. It is very important to note that students considering a web-based, self-paced, or televised course must be very self motivated and disciplined to work in an independent environment.

- **On campus courses:** These are your more traditional, face-to-face courses. They may also utilize a web-based component to some extent. Check your catalog for this component.
- **Web based courses:** Web-based courses are delivered via the Internet. To participate in a web-based course, students need basic computer skills and access to a computer with an Internet connection. TCC's computer labs can be used to participate in online courses.
- **Self-Paced:** These are independent study courses in which students work at their own pace over the 20 weeks required to complete each course. They are not required to attend on-campus classes.
- **Televised:** Televised courses usually have materials available at the campus bookstore. The actual course, however, is delivered over a local television station at a given time. Televised courses often involve on-campus group sessions, including a mandatory orientation meeting.

IDENTIFY WHEN YOU ARE MORE ALERT

One component of your preferred learning environment is the time of day in which you are most alert. The time of day can affect your concentration, attention, and performance both academically and professionally. If you find you are more alert and able to concentrate in the morning, then you will want to take morning classes and schedule your work hours in the afternoon or evening. Remember, while you are in school, your studies should be your first priority! You will want to study and attend class during your peak performance hours.

INTERNAL AND EXTERNAL DISTRACTIONS

Internal distractions are things inside you such as hunger or muscle aches. Depression, anxiety, fatigue, and other distracting feelings are also considered internal distractions. Do you find that being hungry or tired makes it difficult to concentrate? Then you will want to ensure that you get enough sleep and have healthy snack food available while studying.

You will also want to note whether your concentration is affected by *external distractions*. An external distraction is something outside yourself that causes a reaction. The reaction can be positive or negative. Do you study better in a quiet place like a library, or do you prefer background noise? Some people find a messy desk or study area distracting, while others wouldn't be affected. Before even sitting down to study, you will want to ensure that you are in an environment favorable to concentration. Identify any external stimuli that distract you from learning.

IDENTIFY AND CONTROL YOUR EXTERNAL DISTRACTIONS

- **Electronic interruptions.** If interruptions make concentration difficult, turn off your cell phone, close instant messaging and email notification, and any other electronic means for getting in touch with you. Your concentration is broken each time you stop to answer that email, text message, or instant message. This can really impact your ability to study!

- **People talking.** Whether at home, in a bookstore or a coffee shop, sometimes just the soft sound of people can break your concentration. If this is the case, you may want to go to the library to study.

- **Background noise.** While some people may prefer background music or noise, others find it a distraction. Music or television sets don't need to be loud to be distracting. Just the constant background noise can be enough to break one's focus. If this is the case for you, turn off the music or television. If this isn't possible, go to another location to study.

- **Activity around you.** Just knowing that others are nearby, having a good time, or the noise of everyday home activities can affect your concentration. If so, you may want to go to the library or a bookstore to study.

- **Family or friends interrupting your studies.** If family members or roommates make demands on your time when you need to be studying, you may have to study away from home. If, however, you prefer studying at home, let your friends and family know and close the door when you're working. Your friends need to respect your study time! Since they want you to succeed, they will understand that you can't be available all the time.

CONSIDER THE FOLLOWING STUDENT

Sally has just gotten home from a long day of school and work, and she plans to study for a test before dinner. As she sits at her desk and clears space for her books, her roommate starts to watch a movie in the other room. Sally tries to drown out the noise by playing her music louder, and a song begins that reminds her of a conversation she had with a friend earlier. As her mind wanders, she leans back to reflect on the day's events.

What types of distractions are affecting Sally's ability to study? Identify which distractions are external and which are internal. What could Sally do to help eliminate those distractions?

CREATING A PRODUCTIVE STUDY ENVIRONMENT

Where and how you study is a matter of personal preference. Many students feel the need to have absolute quiet in their study areas, while others insist they can't study without music. Some students like to study with others, while many prefer solitude. By now you've probably established a study pattern, but everyone's study habits can be improved. As you evaluate your own study habits, consider:

- **Study Location.** Having a designated study area helps to put you in "study mode." You may prefer a desk in your bedroom, the library on campus, or the kitchen table. The location you choose should be as free from distractions and/or interruptions as possible.

- **Study Conditions.** Adequate lighting is a must! Overhead lighting or a lamp with good diffused lighting is important. You'll also need a desk or table with adequate writing area, plenty of space for books, and a sturdy, comfortable chair. Remember: If you have a computer, you still need adequate writing space. If you're studying in TCC's Learning Resource Center, the natural light there, combined with the overhead lighting, creates a fine atmosphere for most students.

- **Organizing Your Supplies.** If you study mostly at home, it's easy to organize your study supplies. A bulletin board or corkboard is perfect for posting weekly assignments and the due dates of major projects. Pens, pencils, markers, and highlighters can be kept in a pencil bag or small plastic box if you don't have a desk drawer. Larger supplies, such as folders, notebooks, paper, and reference materials, can be kept in a plastic or cardboard box. Be sure to keep a dictionary and thesaurus at your desk, or bookmark a website (such as http://www.websters.com) that contains them. If you tend to study on campus or in another location, a briefcase or backpack can be fitted with your basic study materials.

LEARNING STYLES

Your *learning style* is your preferred way to acquire new information. It may be any combination of the three learning styles: visual, auditory, and tactile. Your preferred learning style is not the *only* way you can learn; just your preferred way.

Students who have a strong *visual learning style* prefer to use their visual sense. They learn best by reading, demonstrations, videos, images, flash cards, and diagrams. As the learner reads, the information is frequently translated into images. Many textbooks and online courses provide PowerPoint slide shows, images, and games. Check with your instructor to find out if the textbook you are using has any accompanying study aids. In addition, a learner with a strong visual learning style will prefer to study in a well-organized area, free from noise and other distractions.

Visual Learner Study Tips

- **Spelling:** Picture one letter at a time, make a mental picture of the whole word, and then write the word. You might also try flash cards, or visualizing the word, saying it, and then writing it.

- **Problem solving:** Write down or type the problem you are trying to solve, then your thoughts/ideas as they come to you. Don't worry about putting your ideas in any particular order at first. Reread what you have written and organize the ideas under headings and subheadings, looking for possible solutions. If you typed on the computer, it is easy to move the concepts around to organize your ideas.

- **Written instructions:** Large expanses of written instructions can be daunting. When no images are provided, make a rough sketch or diagram of what needs to be done. If pictures or diagrams are provided, visually scan them and then go through the instructions step by step. Try to picture the directions in your mind and make frequent reference to any pictures or diagrams that are provided with each step of the instructions.

- **Reviewing for tests:** Review any PowerPoint slide shows, videos, images, and other multimedia provided with the text or online documents. Review the readings and try to picture any related images or diagrams as you read. If Bill were preparing for a test about the ear, he would review diagrams and then, as he read about the inner ear, he would try to picture a diagram of it as he read about each part.

Having a strong *auditory learning style* means a student learns best from listening to an explanation, verbal instructions, lectures, or books on tape. These students may find that reading aloud instructions, definitions, or passages from a textbook helps them learn new material. They will prefer to study in an area that is free from outside noises, such as conversations, the television, and loud music.

Auditory Learner Study Tips

- **Spelling:** Say the word aloud, sound it out phonically, and then spell the word aloud. Use the word in a sentence, say the word, and then spell it again.

- **Problem solving:** State the problem aloud, then try and reason out the problem verbally to yourself or another person. Write down the key points that must be covered and ensure that you can verbally explain them. If you can explain something clearly to another person, then you truly have a grasp of it! Look at any diagram or pictures describing a problem, and then explain how to resolve it using the images as a starting point.

- **Written instructions:** Read the instructions aloud before attempting to follow them. If you are in public, talk as softly as possible, but be sure to read the instructions aloud to yourself.

- **Reviewing for tests:** After reading a section in your textbook or online lectures, summarize it aloud. Read your notes aloud. Make lists of key terms and explain the concepts aloud. Always take advantage of listening to any audio or audio/video files provided by your instructor or textbook. Review drawings, diagrams, and images, then explain them verbally. You might consider writing key concepts and then reading aloud what you have written.

Students with a strong *tactile (kinesthetic) learning style* prefer learning that involves the tactile (touching) sense, such as hands-on activities, interactive games, and tutorials. While reading and learning key concepts, the tactile learner will benefit from using objects to represent concepts, flash cards, and getting up and moving around to think about concepts. Since these students find action and touching important to learning, it can be difficult for them to concentrate for long periods of time. Simply sitting and reading is not the way this learner prefers to study!

Tactile Learner Study Tips

- **Spelling:** Write the words or create flash cards. You might also have another person quiz you and you can use the letters from a Scrabble game to spell out the words.

- **Problem solving:** When problem solving, use objects to represent ideas. Then write down the steps for resolving the problem. Try sketching out the problem with diagrams, arrows, and explanations.

- **Written instruction:** Use a highlighter to draw attention to important pieces of text that you need to remember. With pen in hand, make notes in the margin as you read or take notes on a sheet of paper so that you will remember the key terms and items you have read.

- **Reviewing for tests:** Get up and move around frequently, and use hands-on activities to learn whenever possible. See if your textbook or instructors have provided interactive games or PowerPoint slide shows for review. List items on your fingers or use objects to represent items. Try cutting diagrams or pictures into pieces that you must then put back together. While learning about the ear, you might cut an image of the ear in pieces and regroup the pieces one at a time. As you put it back together, either write or verbally explain each piece.

EXERCISE:
ADAPTING TO LEARNING ENVIRONMENTS

1. Reflect on the classes in which you performed well. What did you like about the courses? Do you feel there was a relationship between your performance and the learning environment? Was your preferred learning style met? If so, explain.

2. How might you adapt to a learning environment in which your instructor teaches in a way that doesn't meet your preferred learning style?

Now that you have reflected upon what type of learner you think you might be, take the following assessment that will tell you where you fall in the learning style spectrum.

LEARNING STYLE MODALITY PREFERENCE INVENTORY

Read each statement and select the appropriate number response as it applies to you.

3 = Often   2 = Sometimes   1 = Seldom/Never

A:

_____ I remember information better if I write it down.
_____ Looking at the person helps keep me focused.
_____ I need a quiet place to get my work done.
_____ When I take a test, I can see the textbook page in my head.
_____ I need to write down directions, not just take them verbally.
_____ Music or background noise distracts my attention from the task at hand.
_____ I don't always get the meaning of a joke.
_____ I doodle and draw pictures on the margins of my notebook pages.
_____ I have trouble following lectures.
_____ I react very strongly to colors.
_____ **Total**

B:

_____ My papers and notebooks always seem messy.
_____ When I read, I need to use my index finger to track my place on the line.
_____ I don't follow written directions well.
_____ If I hear something, I will remember it.
_____ Writing has always been difficult for me.
_____ I often misread words for the text (i.e., then for than).
_____ I would rather listen and learn than read and learn.
_____ I'm not very good at interpreting an individual's body language.
_____ Pages with small print or poor quality copies are difficult for me to read.
_____ My eyes tire quickly, even though my vision checkup is always fine.
_____ **Total**

C:

_____ I start a project before reading the directions.
_____ I hate to sit at a desk for long periods of time.
_____ I prefer first to see something done and then do it myself.
_____ I use the trial-and-error approach to problem solving.
_____ I like to read my textbook while riding an exercise bike.
_____ I take frequent study breaks.
_____ I have a difficult time giving step-by-step instructions.
_____ I enjoy and do well at several different types of sports.
_____ I use my hands when describing things.
_____ I have to rewrite or type my class notes to reinforce the material.
_____ **Total**

Scoring Instructions

Total the score for each section. A score of 21 points or more in a modality indicates a strength in the area. The highest of the three scores indicates the most efficient method of information intake. The second-highest score indicates the modality that boosts the primary strength.

___ A = Visual Modality Score   ___ B = Auditory Modality Score   ___ C =Tactile/Kinesthetic Modality Score

MULTIPLE INTELLIGENCE—WHAT DOES IT MEAN FOR YOU?

Dr. Howard Gardner, a psychologist and professor at Harvard University, is one of many researchers who have studied how people learn and what makes them successful in school and in life. His theory that there are multiple ways a person can be intelligent might help you understand your own abilities. While most people have all of the intelligences, a couple of them are usually more developed than the others. Tapping into your strongest intelligences to learn new material will help you understand and master it more readily. Think of them as special talents. If you are talented in a certain area, doesn't that usually mean that it is easier to learn and perform in that area? That's what the multiple intelligence theory is all about. So far Dr. Gardner has identified eight different kinds of intelligence that are outlined below.

Verbal/Linguistic—relates to written and spoken words. People who are good at reading, writing, speaking, debating, or learning foreign languages have a high level of this type of intelligence. The ACT, SAT, IQ tests, and/or other standardized tests taken in school have parts that measure verbal ability. High scores on these tests are considered accurate predictors of college success because verbal ability is one of the two kinds of intelligence emphasized in school. Those who have this type of intelligence fit our traditional notions of "smart."

Logical/Mathematical—has to do with reasoning, critical thinking, problem solving, recognizing patterns, and working with abstract symbols such as numbers or geometric shapes. This is the other type of intelligence that is measured by virtually all standardized tests and is usually the ticket to college success and a good job. Schools place the utmost importance on teaching and developing this intelligence in students. Science, math, and computer science majors usually have high levels of logical/mathematical intelligence.

Visual/Spatial—relies on eyesight and also the ability to visualize things/places. Those in our culture who appreciate the visual arts such as painting, drawing, and sculpture value it. This intelligence is useful in situations where you need to be able to use space or get around and include such areas as in navigation, map-making, architecture, computer-aided drafting, graphic arts, and so forth. It is also an ability that is used in games or puzzles where seeing things from different angles is an advantage. People with strong visual/spatial intelligence can look at something and see how it could be improved or see beyond what *is* to what *could be*. This intelligence is often considered synonymous with a good imagination.

Bodily/Kinesthetic—the ability to express oneself through movement or to do things using the body, or to make things. This intelligence is seen in athletes, dancers, actors/actresses, artists, skilled craftspeople, and inventors. People with this intelligence are often very physically active. The ability to use the capabilities of one's body, sometimes even without conscious thought, is another characteristic of this intelligence.

Musical/Rhythmic—being able to "tune in" to sounds and rhythms and use them to create mood changes in the brain. For example, creating soothing melodies, stirring marches, or stimulating raps requires strong use of this intelligence. Expressing yourself with sounds from nature, musical instruments, or the human voice or being able to differentiate tone qualities are more examples of this intelligence. Often people with this intelligence enjoy listening to music as they work on other things or seem to have an "ear" for it. Unfortunately, this intelligence is often not emphasized in school curriculums and is an "extra" that usually gets cut from tight budgets, even though research has shown that learning to play an instrument stimulates connectors in the brain that enhance other learning. Music and rhythm make up a universal language that can transcend culture and touch people's lives. This can be a powerful intelligence to develop.

Interpersonal—the capacity to communicate effectively with others through verbal and nonverbal expression. Persons who have a high degree of this intelligence can work effectively in groups. They notice and understand things about other people such as their moods, facial expressions, posture, gestures, inner motivations, and personality types. They can also listen to others and make them feel valuable and appreciated. Although teachers like students to get along, children with a naturally high level of interpersonal intelligence may have gotten in trouble for being "too social" in school. Though it is invaluable in many occupations, people who have this talent are often drawn into the helping professions.

Intrapersonal—probably the least understood and/or valued in our educational system, this intelligence deals with knowing and understanding oneself. It involves being able to analyze our own thinking and problem solving processes, being aware of our inner thoughts, feelings, and internal state. It is also a sensitivity to and understanding of spiritual realities, and experiencing wholeness and unity as a person. Being able to anticipate the future and contemplate our unrealized potential requires this type of intelligence. Because people with high levels of this intelligence enjoy solitude, meditation, and quiet, their abilities may not be recognized. They probably don't mind, though. Their self-concept and self-confidence does not come from what others think of them. They set their own goals and agendas and know exactly why they do and say the things they do.

Naturalistic—the ability to live in harmony with the natural world and appreciate nature. People who have a "green thumb," or a "way with animals," or who could survive in the wilderness without modern conveniences have naturalistic intelligence. It also includes people who are perceptive about differences in the natural world such as being able to recognize the many kinds of flowers, trees, birds, and can use this ability productively. Farmers, biological scientists, and hunters might utilize naturalistic intelligence. In addition, Dr. Gardner believes that people in our materialistic, consumer culture display naturalistic intelligence when they can distinguish even subtle differences among car styles, athletic shoes, and the like.

When you read these descriptions, can you pick out your strongest type of intelligence from Gardner's list? What do you think would happen if our school systems actually taught in ways that emphasized all of the intelligences? Even though the traditional ways of being smart have always been a pathway to success, it is interesting to note that the types of intelligence least emphasized by schools in the United States, when developed fully, provide some of the greatest income potential and social status. Professional athletes, entertainers, musicians, actors, actresses, and artists have a lot more visibility in our society than doctors, judges, scientists, or mathematicians.

Directions: Read each statement carefully and thoroughly. After reading the statement, rate your response using the scale below. There are no right or wrong answers. This is not a timed survey. The MIS is based, in part, on *Frames of Mind* by Howard Gardner, 1983.

3 = Often Applies   2 = Sometimes Applies   1 = Never or Almost Never Applies

_____ 1. When someone gives me directions, I have to visualize them in my mind in order to understand them.

_____ 2. I enjoy crossword puzzles and word games like Scrabble.

_____ 3. I enjoy dancing and can keep up with the beat of the music.

_____ 4. I have little or no trouble conceptualizing information or facts.

_____ 5. I like to repair things that are broken such as toasters, small engines, bicycles, and cars.

_____ 6. I enjoy leadership activities on campus and in the community.

_____ 7. I have the ability to get others to listen to me.

_____ 8. I enjoy working with nature, animals, and plants.

_____ 9. I know where everything is in my home such as supplies, gloves, flashlights, camera, and compact discs.

_____ 10. I am a good speller.

_____ 11. I often sing or hum to myself in the shower or car, or while walking or just sitting.

_____ 12. I am a very logical, orderly thinker.

_____ 13. I use a lot of gestures when I talk to people.

_____ 14. I can recognize and empathize with people's attitudes and emotions.

_____ 15. I prefer to study alone.

_____ 16. I can name many different things in the environment such as clouds, rocks, and plant types.

_____ 17. I like to draw pictures, graphs, or charts to better understand information.

_____ 18. I have a good memory for names and dates.

_____ 19. When I hear music, I "get into it" by moving, humming, tapping, or even singing.

_____ 20. I learn better by asking a lot of questions.

_____ 21. I enjoy playing competitive sports.

_____ 22. I communicate very well with other people.

_____ 23. I know what I want and I set goals to accomplish it.

_____ 24. I have some interest in herbal remedies and natural medicine.

_____ 25. I enjoy working puzzles or mazes.

_____ 26. I am a good story teller.

_____ 27. I can easily remember the words and melodies of songs.

_____ 28. I enjoy solving problems in math and chemistry and working with computer programming problems.

_____ 29. I usually touch people or pat them on the back when I talk to them.

_____ 30. I understand my family and friends better than most other people do.

_____ 31. I don't always talk about my accomplishments with others.

_____ 32. I would rather work outside around nature than inside around people and equipment.

_____ 33. I enjoy and learn more when seeing movies, slides, or videos in class.

_____ 34. I am a good listener and I enjoy listening to others' stories.

_____ 35. I need to study with music.

_____ 36. I enjoy games like Clue, Battleship, Chess, and Rubik's Cube.

_____ 37. I enjoy physical activities such as bicycling, jogging, dancing, snowboarding, skateboarding, or swimming.

_____ 38. I am good at solving people's problems and conflicts.

_____ 39. I have to have time alone to think about new information in order to remember it.

_____ 40. I enjoy sorting and organizing information, objects, and collectibles.

Refer to your score on each individual question. Place that score beside the appropriate question number below. Then, tally each line at the side.

SCORE					TOTAL ACROSS	CODE
1_____	9_____	17_____	25_____	33_____	_____	Visual/Spatial
2_____	10_____	18_____	26_____	34_____	_____	Verbal/Linguistic
3_____	11_____	19_____	27_____	35_____	_____	Musical/Rhythm
4_____	12_____	20_____	28_____	36_____	_____	Logic/Math
5_____	13_____	21_____	29_____	37_____	_____	Body/Kinesthetic
6_____	14_____	22_____	30_____	38_____	_____	Interpersonal
7_____	15_____	23_____	31_____	39_____	_____	Intrapersonal
8_____	16_____	24_____	32_____	40_____	_____	Naturalistic

MIS TALLY
Multiple Intelligence

Look at these scores on the MIS. What are your top three scores? Write them in the space below.

Top Score _____   Code_____

Second Score _____   Code_____

Third Score _____   Code_____

This tally can help you understand where some of your strengths may be. Again, this is not a measure of your worth or capabilities, nor is it an indicator of your future successes.

Now that you have an idea of your MIS let's take it a step further. Selecting a major area of study will be one of your most important academic decisions. Take a few moments to reflect on the connection between majors and careers. The middle column of the following chart correlates each multiple intelligence with a handful of associated careers. Complete the final column—"What Major will Prepare you for these Careers?".

MULTIPLE INTELLIGENCE, CAREERS AND MAJORS

MULTIPLE INTELLIGENCE	POSSIBLE CAREERS	WHAT MAJORS WILL PREPARE YOU FOR THESE CAREERS?
Linguistics Intelligence (Word Smart)	Writer, Public speaker, Lawyer, Teacher, Journalist, Librarian, Talk show host, Tour guide	
Logical—Mathematical Intelligence (Number Smart)	Scientist, Mathematician, Banker, Investment broker, Accountant, Doctor	
Spatial Intelligence (Art Smart)	Sculptor, Painter, Anatomy, Teacher, Architect, Builder, Photographer, Urban planner, Artist	
Bodily—Kinesthetic Intelligence (Body Smart)	Athlete, Actor, Dancer, Trainer, Gymnast, Massage therapist, Model	
Musical Intelligence (Music Smart)	Musician, Dancer, Critic, Music instructor, Singer, Record producer	
Interpersonal Intelligence (People Smart)	Teacher, Politician, Salesperson, Arbitrator, Manager, Human resources executive, Psychologist, Social worker, Marriage counselor, Coach	
Intrapersonal Intelligence (Me Smart)	Independent-type work, Lifestyle coach, Energy healer, Clergy, Philosopher, Writer	
Naturalist Intelligence (Nature Smart)	Botanist, Zoologist, Archaeologist, Meteorologist, Environmentalist, Animal trainer, Veterinarian	

SUMMARY

You must make a conscious effort to know what *learning styles* and environments are best for you personally. Your preferred learning style is not the only way that you can study, nor is it the only way you *should* study. Depending on the material, different styles or a combination of styles may work better. Having also looked at the different personal assessments presented in this chapter, you should now have a better idea of what makes you you and how to best exploit this knowledge so that you are in a learning environment and ultimately a career you love. In the next couple of chapters you will learn about how to use your knowledge of your personal learning style to have a better experience both inside the classroom and beyond its walls.

Using the proper study methods includes finding and using a good *study environment*. Identify how your *internal* and *external stimuli* impact your learning. A good study environment is free of distractions and encourages you to concentrate on the material in front of you. Distractions come in many forms, and some are more subtle than others. Too much noise around you, being tired or hungry, or thinking about your day are all distractions that can hinder your ability to study and learn.

Chapter 9

Don't Forget . . .
Memory and Concentration

LEARNING OBJECTIVES

By the end of this chapter you should be able to:

Recognize the stages of memory
Understand the three stages of memory
Use strategies designed to help with memory
Realize how memory processing and concentration work together

WHY YOU FORGET

DO YOU EVER wish you could read something once and remember it? Unfortunately, the mind doesn't work that way. One reading of textbook material is seldom enough. Much of the information printed in textbooks will be new to you and you may need several readings to understand and absorb it. Also, you forget most of what you read soon after reading it unless you make a conscious effort to remember it. Finally, if you want to retain information, you must periodically review what you have read.

Forgetting is not only normal; it's also necessary. If you never forgot anything, your mind would be so crammed with useless information that you wouldn't be able to think. Do you remember what your phone number was in every place you have lived? You probably don't. Information that you cease to use soon passes out of your memory unless it has special significance. *Your mind remembers only what you need and discards the rest.* In fact, when you learn something new, forgetting starts within an hour. After several days, you remember very little of the new information unless you take action to prevent forgetting.

WHAT IS MEMORY?

Memory is the brain's ability to store and access information that has been acquired through life experiences. Effective use of memory is essential for critical thinking, perception, problem solving, learning, and language.

TYPES OF MEMORY

Memory is the brain's *information-processing* system, and can be divided into three general categories: sensory memory, short-term memory, and long-term memory.

Sensory memory deals with information received through your five senses: sight, hearing, touch, smell, and taste. Your brain is constantly taking in information via your five senses. However, you don't need all that data, so your brain doesn't store it in long-term memory. Sensory memory is discarded from memory after only a few seconds.

Consider: You park your car at the mall and walk in. Can you then remember the colors of every car you passed on your way? No, of course not. You have to *decide* you want to remember before any information will be stored in either your short-term or long-term memory. That's why it's so important that you make the conscious decision to learn and pay attention in class.

Haven't you ever been in a class or meeting, listening, only to realize afterward that you can't recall a thing that was discussed? Although the information was coming in via your senses, your concentration on the speaker and presentation was minimal. You might have been day-dreaming, checking your email, whispering to the person beside you, or listening to music on your MP3 player.

Being an active listener and taking notes on what you hear will help you understand and retain the key points of a presentation. By adding writing, another sensory input, you are assisting your brain in identifying data to move to your short-term memory. This process, called *selective attention*, allows the brain to determine whether the information it's receiving is important enough to transfer to the next stage, short-term memory.

Short-term memory includes all the information currently being processed in a person's brain and it's generally thought to have a very limited capacity (**30–60 seconds**). It is also very limited in its capacity and cannot store a large amount of data. For example, when you look up the phone number for a pizza delivery, you use your short-term memory to store the number long enough to dial. But, if 45 minutes later, you want to call back because the pizza still hasn't been delivered, you will probably need to look up the number again.

Long-term memory is where the information that you can access and use at a later time is kept: facts, names, key numbers, personal experiences, and skills such as cooking, playing a musical instrument, and using a computer. You can keep an enormous amount of information in your long-term memory. What is critical is being able to retrieve that information! Typically, people are able to remember something if they have already had to retrieve it, especially recently, or if it is associated with a related and recently accessed memory.

THE THREE STAGES OF MEMORY

Memory is a three stage process of acquiring information, moving information from sensory memory through short-term and into long-term memory, and accessing that information again when you need it. These three stages are called encoding, storage, and retrieval. Slightly over-simplifying, these three stages can be referred to as getting it, keeping it, and finding it again.

Encoding: Get It

First, you must notice and pay attention to something—you cannot remember what you never learn. You have to *decide* you want to remember before any information will move from sensory memory and be stored in either your short-term or long-term memory. That's why it's so important that you make the conscious decision to learn and pay attention in class.

Being an active listener and taking notes on what you hear will help you understand and retain the key points of a presentation. By adding writing, another sensory input, you are assisting your brain in identifying data to move to your short-term memory. If you make an active decision to pay attention, you are far more likely to be able to remember later.

> *Consider the way a student named Abdul deals with his daily mail. For a while he didn't have a mailbox and he couldn't receive any mail at all. When he finally did get mail, he would usually let it pile up for several days before he even looked at it. Much of what arrived in the box was "junk"—unimportant things he didn't need to pay any attention to. Unfortunately, sometimes he missed seeing important items like bills.*

Storage: Keep It

Second, you must retain the information in your brain—much of what we notice we immediately forget. We all forget at times. But by reciting aloud names, numbers, and other small pieces of information, you'll help your brain retain them. Have you ever been on your way out the door to do some shopping when a family member asks you to pick something up from the store? And when you're done with your own shopping, you can't remember what you were asked to get? Next time, try reciting your shopping list aloud three or four times. Recitation can also help you remember new names. When you're first introduced to a person, use his or her name in greeting, then as you talk, and again when you say goodbye. It's really true that if you use the name at least three times during the conversation you'll remember it longer! That's because saying the person's name uses another of your senses, speech, and thus increases your chance of retaining the information.

There is evidence to suggest that you can remember **five to nine items of information,** such as numbers or words. However, you can also store information in meaningful "chunks," which increases the amount you can retain. If you concentrate on remembering each group of numbers, letters, or words, you can recall more data. Do you have difficulty remembering long numbers, such as your driver's license or credit card number? Try *chunking* the information by breaking the material into small groups of items to help retain the information in your short-term memory.

- 18509249931 could be split to resemble a phone number: 1 850 924 9931
- IWS12*IGAD can be expanded into a sentence:
  I WILL SUCCEED 12* IN GETTING A DEGREE

MEMORY STRATEGIES

There are many strategies for effective retrieval of long-term memories. These are some of the strategies students find most helpful:

- **Get interested.** Try to relate the topic to something you are interested in or to an aspect of your own life.
- **Be an active listener/reader.** More than anything, you must be motivated to learn and make a conscious effort to retain what you learn. As you read a textbook or listen to a lecture, remind yourself that you need to remember what you are reading or hearing. Review the chapter to be covered ahead of time so that you can decide what is important; then spend your efforts in class on remembering what you really need to know.
- **Take every opportunity to use self-assessment tests and memory games.** Many instructors employ games, such as flash cards and crossword puzzles, and methods to assess your own progress—all of which aid you in retaining key information. Studies show that frequent testing enhances your long-term recall much better than studying as an end in itself.
- **Use as many of your senses as possible to learn and retain information.** This includes reciting, writing down the points you want to remember, listening to audio and video files, and reviewing images and diagrams.
- **Organize the material in a way that makes it easier to learn.** Develop course material into outlines, lists, or another form that allows you to relate each item to the others. Once you can fill in part of a list with a few items the rest are easier to retrieve from memory. Create diagrams, charts, or sketches to help you visualize the connections. Not only does this show how the items relate, but also provides you with a single-page document for use as a review sheet.
- **Use key words.** A single word or two can help you retrieve additional information.
- **Summarize the material.** A brief summary is easier to retain and can help you retrieve more information from long-term memory.
- **Use frequent, short study sessions.** Short study sessions of 45 minutes to an hour, followed by a 15-minute break, work better than an uninterrupted 3-hour stretch.

Memorization Techniques

There are many techniques to learn and retain information, commonly known as **memory devices**, but you'll have to find those that work best for you. A mnemonic technique that's easy for one person may be harder for another. Some techniques may also be better suited to learning specific types of information. The key to efficient learning is to use multiple techniques when memorizing new material.

- **Mnemonics.** The use of tricks, games, or rhymes to help you remember. For example: In 1492 Columbus sailed the ocean blue.

- **Rhyming.** A simple rhyming phrase or song can help you remember something that may be difficult to memorize or difficult to recall. For example:
    - "Righty tighty, lefty loosey" to remember which way to tighten a screw.
    - Stalag*mites* where the letter **G** stands for ground, and stala*ctites* where the letter **C** stands for ceiling.
    - The "ABC" song.

- **Acronyms.** An acronym is a word that has been formed from the first letter of other words. Acronyms can be very useful memory aids for memorizing words in a specific order, but do not aid you in developing an understanding of the material. Some examples of common acronyms include PC (personal computer) and NBA (National Basketball Association). To remember the Great Lakes (Huron, Ontario, Michigan, Erie, Superior), one can just remember the acronym HOMES. What other acronyms can you think of?

- **Acrostics.** Acrostics are text or poems in which the first letter, syllable, or word of each sentence, paragraph, or other recurring feature spells out another message. You can rearrange the letters and words in any order you wish. *Maybe Robert Ate All of his Apple while Visiting Rick* is an example of an acrostic sentence, taken from the first letters of *Mnemoics, Rhyming, Acronyms, Acrostics, Associations, Visualize,* and *Repetition.*

- **Associations.** To help you retain a new piece of information, try to associate it with something else that you already know. The assumption is that if the new information is tied to a piece of prior, familiar information, you will have an easier time remembering and retrieving the memory.

- **Visualize.** Make a mental picture of what you want to remember. Do you need to know the parts of the inner ear? Look at the picture; then close your eyes and try to form a mental image of the inner ear. This is an excellent way to master maps and diagrams. It can also be a fun way to memorize a list of words or items: make a mental image of each and of how they relate to one another.

- **Repetition.** While strict repetition for memorization is not an easy or efficient way to learn new information, it is sometimes the only choice. Whenever possible, try to combine this form of memorization with word associations, key words, or mnemonics.

EXERCISE: PRACTICE USING CHUNKING

1. Write an example of chunking to remember an item from one of your classes or personal life (do not use a phone number or credit card number).

    _____

    _____

    _____

> *Again consider Abdul and his mail. Once the pile of mail got too big to ignore, Abdul would sit down and read through all of it, opening every envelope, and looking at every flyer. This would take a long time, which only made him want to put it off longer. Frequently, Adbul would come across old bills that were overdue by the time he even opened them, and thus he had to pay late fees on top of the bills. Once he had finished going through the mail and paying the bills, Abdul would gather up the whole pile of paper and put it in the recycling bin.*

Retrieval: Find It Again

Third, you must be able to access the memory when you want it. Have you ever had the experience of an answer being "right on the tip of your tongue," but unable to actually say it? What is critical is being able to retrieve that information! Typically, people are able to remember something if they have already had to retrieve it, especially recently, or if it is associated with a related and recently accessed memory.

That means you must focus attention on the information, consider its meaning, and relate it to other data already stored in long-term memory. And you must work at recalling course-related content in order to have those memories available when you need them. For instance, if you learned a concept at the very beginning of the semester and then did not review it for the final, you may very well not be able to access the memory during the exam. This is where note taking, having a study system, reviewing your notes, and developing your test-taking skills will help you retain and access the material stored in your long-term memory.

> *Once again, consider Abdul and his mail. Suppose he realizes he needs to keep some important papers, so he decides to put all the important papers from the mail into a box labeled "important." Just knowing that he has the documents is not nearly as useful as being able to find them quickly. Although he could easily find papers he had used recently, after a while Abdul will start to lose track of what he put where. Using an organizational system, for example an expandable folder with pockets, would help Abdul quickly find things after a longer time has passed. This will also help him to ensure that he knows where important papers are when he needs them.*

Impairments to Long-Term Memory

Your physical and mental condition can impair your brain's ability to store information in long-term memory. Included are factors such as depression, the use of drugs or alcohol, and a lack of motivation or attention. Most of us have experienced how some medications can cause us to become sleepy or unable to focus! The use of over-the-counter cold or flu pills, to say nothing of illegal drugs and alcohol, can have a negative impact on your ability to pay attention during class or transfer information from short-term to long-term memory. If you can't pay attention in class, the information presented there probably won't make it past your sensory memory. Depression and lack of motivation can have the same result. Talk with your teacher or counselor if you are experiencing such difficulties.

EXERCISE: PRACTICE USING ACROSTICS

1. Write a sentence (acrostics) to remember content from one of your classes.

    _____

    _____

    _____

2. Write a sentence (acrostics) to remember several of the main points of this chapter.

    _____

    _____

    _____

These techniques are useful for memorizing straight facts, but don't necessarily help you grasp an overall concept. It's helpful to have a general understanding of the material and ideas that you're trying to learn before attempting to memorize select facts from that material. By preparing ahead, you can build better associations when using mnemonic techniques. And naturally, you'll also find that it's much easier to memorize the material once you understand it.

While studying, you should quiz yourself periodically to ensure that you remember what you're currently memorizing as well as what you've already memorized. You will, of course, forget some of the material over time and as you concentrate on new information. However, by reviewing previously learned material, you'll recall it more readily and retain it longer.

MEMORY PROCESSING

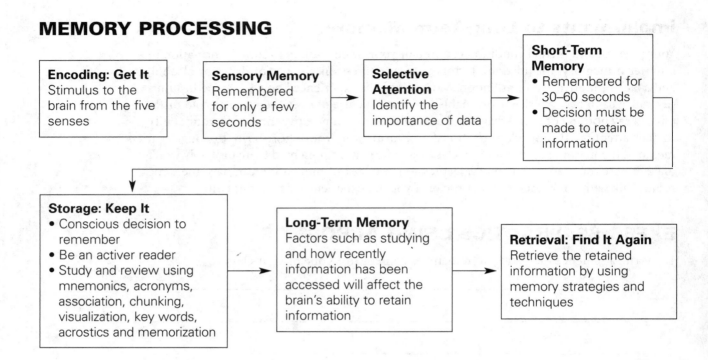

Encoding: Get It
Stimulus to the brain from the five senses

Sensory Memory
Remembered for only a few seconds

Selective Attention
Identify the importance of data

Short-Term Memory
• Remembered for 30–60 seconds
• Decision must be made to retain information

Storage: Keep It
• Conscious decision to remember
• Be an activer reader
• Study and review using mnemonics, acronyms, association, chunking, visualization, key words, acrostics and memorization

Long-Term Memory
Factors such as studying and how recently information has been accessed will affect the brain's ability to retain information

Retrieval: Find It Again
Retrieve the retained information by using memory strategies and techniques

Concentration

While it's important to know how your memory works and what techniques can support it, you must also actively concentrate on memorization. *Concentration* involves devoting yourself fully to studying and remembering, not thinking of anything else while doing so. The proper environment is crucial to concentration and memorization.

This idea of concentration is one that we have visited before in this class, though you may not have recognized it as such. When we discussed internal and external distractions, active listening, and learning styles, these things are also a part of the process of memory and concentration. Practicing good techniques will go a long way to help your concentration. Another good way to practice concentration is through games such as *Concentration*, *Trivial Pursuit*, and *Memory* and through Sodoku and crossword puzzles.

You should avoid as many distractions in your environment as possible. These include music, ambient noises such as background conversations and passing cars, and interruptions from family and friends. You should also avoid lying down or lounging in a chair that is too comfortable or you may fall asleep. Sitting at a table or desk is ideal. Before you sit down to study, think about the materials you may need. Lay those materials on the table in front of you, so that if you need them you will not have to stop later.

Short breaks during studying and memorization will help you concentrate longer without tiring. Try to get up and stretch or move for a few minutes while you let your mind and body relax. If you try to study or memorize new material for too long without a break, you may find yourself forgetting it as quickly as you take it in. Pages you just read now seem as unfamiliar as if you hadn't studied at all! Studying periodically, not just cramming everything into one night, will make memorization much easier and benefit you in the long run. You'll find that it takes less time and effort to review the material before a test, which will leave you more time for other activities.

SUMMARY

Memorization and learning are not easy or effortless. You must concentrate fully on what you're trying to learn and engage as many of your senses as possible (e.g., speaking while you write). You may feel that you have a hard time memorizing, but that can be changed. There are many mnemonic techniques that can be used to enhance your recall. If you actively decide to learn and remember information, use the techniques in this chapter, and work in an environment conducive to studying, you'll find your memory strengthening over time. You may even find that it becomes second nature to remember new information and surprise yourself with how much you can remember!

Chapter 10

Mastering the Classroom

LEARNING OBJECTIVES

By the end of this chapter you should be able to:

Identify and list note-taking systems and techniques

Understand the importance of classroom participation

Understand how to facilitate successful group work for projects and presentations

College students need a solid foundation of skills to succeed in the classroom. This chapter will help you develop those skills and the strategies to maximize them at Tallahassee Community College. We will look at the following areas:

- Note-taking strategies
- Collaborative learning skills
- Group projects

PREPARING FOR CLASS AND STUDY STRATEGIES

As a student, you may have wonderful skills and technique, but if you're not prepared for class, the chances are greater that you won't succeed. It's impossible to overstate the importance of having your textbook to accompany the lecture, your pen and paper to take good notes, and your planner and syllabus to schedule homework and tests as the instructor assigns them. Some students don't bring their textbooks to class, missing out on a wonderful resource to accompany the lecture. Always bring your book! And even if attendance isn't mandatory in one of your classes, showing up and being on time will keep you on top of your game.

Your most important tool is the course syllabus, which will keep you on track and help you plan ahead. The syllabus is your main source of information about the course assignments and their due dates. Keep your syllabus, notes, handouts, and other course materials in a folder or three-ring binder and always bring it with you to class. And, keep plenty of blank paper and extra pens for note-taking.

This chapter is designed to help you with studying in the classroom by giving you a sense of what you need to do and providing note-taking strategies for in class. After this we will look at how to take what you learn in class and study it so that you can do well on your tests and in the class.

NOTE TAKING STRATEGIES

Notes provide a useful, convenient record for study and review. Properly used, they are an important reference tool and study supplement. With clear and complete notes, you can identify key lecture points and integrate them into your understanding of the subject. You can also use them to develop and practice exam questions for your review. In this course, for instance, you'll use your notes to learn about the nature of careers, compare and contrast occupations, and analyze your personal strengths and weaknesses. In an interview setting, your notes will remind you to ask the questions most meaningful to you. Taking notes also helps you determine whether the answers you've received are satisfactory; perhaps you'll need to gather more information.

Tips for Strengthening Your Note-Taking Skills

Tip 1

Organize and plan your approach to note-taking. What will you write with? Come to class prepared with several pens or pencils. Black ink is usually best, since it's a dark color, easy to see, and doesn't fade. Ink lasts longer than pencil marks. Remember: You'll be more receptive to studying when your notes are legible.

What will you write on? Where will you keep your notes? Have a separate notebook or binder for each subject. Leave the front pages clean so that you'll have space to create and expand a table of contents as the semester develops. Number all the pages so that you'll have an orderly progression. If you prefer, use a sectioned ring binder to which you can add loose-leaf pages for each subject.

Leave space in your notes to add information and explanatory details.

Tip 2

Take an active role in note-taking. Be an ACTIVE LISTENER. Turn your reading and your instructor's lecture titles or opening sentences into questions—not questions to ask your instructor—but, rather, to plan your listening. Make up your own questions and then listen for the answers.

Pay attention to the instructor's organization and major points. Jot down the ideas as you grasp them. Get in the habit of listening for key concepts and conclusions; identify them and the connections among them. Identify those general assertions that must be supported by specific examples. Identify the supporting details. Information presented to you in a series or a sequence is frequently worthy of note (e.g., "There are four reasons this occurs . . .").

Active listeners pay attention to what they hear and try to make sense of it. Ignore distractions and keep your focus on the material the lecturer is presenting.

Tip 3

Develop your own abbreviations for commonly used words. Your personal shorthand will save time and make sense when you review your notes. For example, psychology may be abbreviated as "psy." You're already familiar with many abbreviations: days of the week, months of the year, states, college courses, etc. You can also use abbreviations from your math studies, such as = (equal to); > (greater than); and < (less than).

There are times when you shouldn't use shorthand. When you are given a precise definition, make sure you record exactly what is presented. This also applies when you are given a formula or an example of the formula's application.

Tip 4

Identify the main ideas. Lecturers sometimes announce the purpose of a lecture or offer an outline, thus providing you with the skeleton of main ideas and details. Use this information to structure your notes, identifying the major points and the details that support them.

During the lecture, many clues indicate that some is more important than other information. Lecturers often change their tone of voice, stamp the podium, or repeat themselves with each key idea. If your instructor emphasizes an idea repeatedly, it should be obvious he or she considers it important. Chances are good you'll see it on the exam. Instructors also ask questions to promote classroom discussion—another clue to what he or she considers important.

Tip 5

Bring your textbooks to class as supportive material. Most instructors refer in their lectures to material in the textbook. Sometimes they'll ask you to do an exercise from the text or to interpret a graph or other visual to accompany the lecture. If you have your text with you, you'll be able to follow along and note important material. Certainly, key to reinforcing your understanding is to use multiple tools and senses.

Tip 6

Make a personal commitment to learn and use good note-taking skills. Assume personal responsibility. A positive frame of mind will strengthen your motivation to be an active listener. Assume that you'll learn something useful, expand your knowledge, and increase your understanding of the course.

Tip 7

Write down what the instructor puts on the board. If the instructor takes the time to write something on the board, give it special consideration.

Tip 8

Write down unfamiliar words and use the dictionary to define them. In class, ask your instructor what unfamiliar words mean. Then learn to use them in your own vocabulary. When you find an unfamiliar term while studying on your own, always look it up (in your dictionary or bookmarked website) before continuing.

Tip 9

Be an active participant. Take notes with a purpose. Summarize statements presented in the lecture, and don't be afraid to ask questions. If you don't understand some of the material, it's likely your classmates have similar concerns.

When you realize you've missed a point, ask the instructor to repeat it. If you don't understand what's being said and need time to consider it, leave a space in your notes and put a question mark (?) there. Fill in voids in your notes by asking a classmate or the instructor after class, certainly before the next class session. You may find graphs, charts, and drawings helpful to your understanding. When these are used to illustrate a point, make your own sketch of what the instructor has presented.

Tip 10

Do not rely on a tape recorder for note-taking. If you use a tape recorder, as is often helpful to auditory learners, don't allow it to make you a passive learner. You'll still need to write down key points and then use the recording to retrieve what you've missed.

Tip 11

Recall. When you take notes, create a recall column on the page. This remains blank while you take notes in class, but should be used within 24 hours to review and integrate (synthesize) your grasp of the material. Write down the main ideas and examples in the recall column.

Tip 12

Recite. Use key words or phrases highlighted in the recall column to remember and recite aloud what you understand from the class notes. This summarization of your notes can then be used to prepare for test-taking.

Tip 13

Review. Before a class, review your syllabus and your notes from the previous day. This is a "warm-up" to help you focus on the material to be covered and think critically during the lecture. Use your notes frequently. Within 24 hours of a lecture, review your notes and complete any information recorded hastily or with the intention of acquiring more detail later.

During this quick trip through your notes, make sure everything is clear and understandable. If not, read your book and check your notes against the text. If you missed some key points, ask other students or your instructor. Or ask the instructor at the beginning of the next class.

Compare and discuss your notes with other students for better retention and understanding. Work on condensing ideas or facts into a few words or phrases that will be meaningful to you later.

Tip 14

Find out who the best note-taker is in your class. Compare notes, borrow notes, restructure notes. If you miss a class, make copies of your classmate's notes, and always return the favor.

Tip 15

Build test questions from your notes. Once you've identified the key points in a lecture, you can anticipate what you'll be asked on a quiz or exam. Make up your own exam questions from the material, just as your instructor does. In a study conducted at one Eastern college, a group of students was asked to use this study method. The result: up to 80% of the actual exam questions were among those the students had prepared ahead of time. In fact, the grades of students using this method were 10 points higher than those of students who didn't (Olney, 1991).

After developing your questions, use your notes to highlight the answers. If you find that an answer is incomplete in your notes, fill in what's missing. You may want to transfer your questions and answers to flash cards for easy and portable review.

Tip 16

Apply your note-taking skills as you study and mark your books.

- Use your pencil as you read.
- Underline important points.
- Write notes in the margins.
- Draw arrows connecting key material.
- Circle material to focus on.
- Find a system of marking your textbook that works for you.

These tips help you to be active in note-taking. They also force you to focus and concentrate on the material. Via active reading and note-taking, you'll consciously search for what is important. Your marks in the textbook serve a purpose similar to that of the recall column; the underlined text provides supporting detail.

The benefits of good note-taking include:

- increased immediate learning
- longer attention span
- more interest in the material
- enhanced ability to apply the material

- better retention
- improved notes for later study

It takes time and self-discipline to use a note-taking study system, but it's worth it! As you progress, you'll acquire new listening skills, improve and control your attitude during a lecture, adjust how you format your notes for best results, and cultivate a high standard of performance that ensures you have studied and used your notes well.

Note-Taking Systems

Four formats are suggested to TCC students. You may find others and adapt them to your needs.

"I" notes were developed by Daniel Walther. He suggests that you draw a large capital "I" in the center of a page. Then, identify the main ideas of a lecture or a chapter of your textbook. Place them to the left of the "I." Put major and minor details to the right of the "I." For those who rarely take notes in ANY style and want to be more organized, this is a good, basic format!

Walther also suggests that you create and jot down several questions—*before* leaving the classroom—which the lecturer could ask on a test. Place those questions beneath the "I," at the bottom of the page. You'll be able to predict with 90% accuracy what was important and what could be asked on the next test.

I-Notes Example

	Oct. 24 Tuesday
Topic: Memory	
Memory process (3 stages)	encoding storing retrieving
4 ways of forgetting	Disuse Interference Repression Not Learning in 1st place

3 questions for next test:
   1)
   2)
   3)	

Informal/Indent Outline is an adaptation of the format taught in many high schools. (If you don't recognize it, don't worry; when classes are asked how many members were taught a note-taking style, the response is usually zero!) This method encourages students to listen for main ideas and concepts and place them closest to the left margin, while placing major, then minor details underneath in a staircase descending order. Details and examples would be further indented as given. As with "I" Notes—it helps.

Outline Example

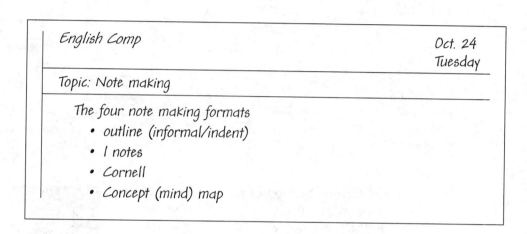

The **Concept Map** or **Mind Map** is a doodler's dream, but a nightmare if you're disorganized. It, too, demands that you listen first for the major concept of the lecture or chapter reading. Then place it in the largest bubble of your notes. Draw parallel concepts and ideas off the main bubble as they're presented. The size of the bubble should be relative to the importance of the idea it contains.

If you have no clue where the lecture is going, for example, how many major concepts will be covered, and then this style of note-taking can be a challenge. It's also difficult to know the relationship of ideas on first hearing, since the oral and written word is generally presented in linear fashion. However, in terms of connecting the concepts LATER, studying the degree of their importance and relationships with each other, this note-taking method can't be beat! To synthesize info for deep processing after class, or to create a personal study guide in preparation for essay writing or tests, it is great. And creating a concept map helps you test yourself before the exam.

Concept (Mind) Map Example

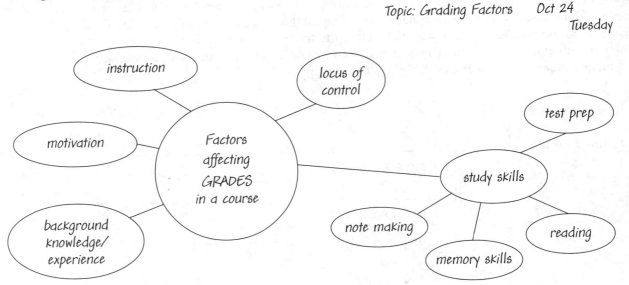

Topic: Grading Factors   Oct 24
Tuesday

The **Cornell Method** of note-taking, devised by Dr. Walter Paulk of Cornell University, is another excellent method. For this system, divide the page into three parts, first by drawing a vertical line 2.5 inches from the left edge of your paper. This creates a wide right-hand and narrow left-hand column. End the line 2 inches above the bottom of the page and draw a horizontal line across the page there. Take your notes in the wide column on the right. On the left, write your questions about the notes. In the 2-inch space along the bottom of the page, summarize your notes.

Now that your paper is set up, these are the steps you should follow in more detail:

1. **Record.** In the wide column, jot down as much of the material as you can. Print if it's more legible for you, use a pen, and write in sentences. As soon as possible after class clarify and complete any errors or omissions in your notes.

2. **Question.** Now, take a few minutes to reread your notes. Then make up questions based on the main ideas. Put these questions in the narrow column on the left, across from the main ideas. Make sure they are broad, "reciting" questions.

3. **Recite.** To recite means to say the information in your own words, aloud, without using your notes. It's such a valuable learning strategy! Not only are you using several of your senses, but you're working for recall as opposed to recognition. Studies show that, when tested 2 weeks later, students who recited could remember 80% of the material, while those who merely reread the material remembered just 20%. Choose your category. If you want to remember 80% (or hopefully even

more), cover up your notes, read the question, and recite your answer. Then take a minute to check your notes again, and recite any information that was left out or incorrect. Continue in this manner through your notes.

4. **Reflect.** For true learning, you'll want to do more than give back information verbatim, so reflection is crucial. In other words, apply what you've learned to your own life. Make it pertinent. Ask yourself how this new information fits in with what you already know. Reflection will make you more enthusiastic and curious about learning. What's more, you'll retain your knowledge longer than you possibly could without this important step.

5. **Review.** Of course, no system could work without reviewing. Review your lecture notes before each class. Plan a time each week to review all lecture notes for every subject. Thanks to your organized note-taking, the review step is all set up for you. Now read the questions aloud, recite the information, double-check the answer, and continue through your questions. Each review will prove you're remembering more information for longer periods of time.

6. **Recapitulate.** This term simply means that you summarize each page of notes at the end of the lecture. This summarizing step requires a higher level of thinking, and will help you to gain a deeper understanding of the material. Dr. Pauk also suggests that you go one step further for optimum learning and summarize the entire lecture on the last note page for that lecture. To be able to summarize will mean that you really got the "meat" of the lecture. It is also a fast and easy way to review just before a test is handed to you.

Cornell Example

Note Making (cont'd)	Cornell Note making method	Oct. 24 Tuesday
24-hour Edit Column (after class) Cue words ← 1/3 page → questions	In-class note-making column ←——— 2/3 page ———→	
Summary	All main ideas All major details Summarized in own words and from memory	

COLLABORATIVE LEARNING SKILLS

Active Learning is a collaborative activity that helps you build interpersonal and communication skills, which help you in the classroom and the rest of your life. Most college instructors welcome and encourage class participation. In many courses, discussion plays a vital role.

Part of learning in the classroom is participating in class discussion; they offer you the chance to examine different perspectives. As mentioned earlier, when information is unclear, you're responsible for asking questions. If you've read your assignment, listened attentively, and still don't understand, then ask the instructor. Most instructors enjoy answering questions, viewing them as a sign of your involvement. If you find it difficult to ask questions in class, talk with the instructor afterward or during office hours.

Seeking clarification is the student's responsibility. Remember: Instructors can't tell by looking at you whether you understand what's being discussed. If you wait to see how you do on the exam, it may be too late!

This active approach applies to other types of class participation. Many professors structure their classes to require participation, which promotes a lively learning environment and allows them to see students in action. While there are students in every class who won't participate (and some who participate without being prepared), most enjoy and benefit from active involvement in the learning process. Needless to say, when participation is a part of the grading system, it's important to contribute during each and every class. While you don't have to talk a lot, do contribute your thoughts and ideas.

Group work is also key to class participation, and playing a productive role in a group means being a team player. Developing outstanding team skills can be a tall order, since teamwork requires a collaborative spirit that doesn't come easily to everyone. Remember, though, that different personalities can contribute in different ways to the team's performance. In fact, they can complement and strengthen each other. You, almost certainly, possess characteristics helpful to your team. Here are some practical steps you can take to build on what you've already developed.

Habits to Cultivate

- Initiate discussions.
- Solicit information and opinions.
- Listen actively.
- Express differences candidly.
- Suggest techniques and strategies for fulfilling mission.
- Clarify ideas.
- Summarize.
- Seek consensus.
- Help team stay focused on task.

Teamwork and Ethics. Chances are you'll be assigned to contribute to a group project before you graduate. You might not care for the assignment or for your teammates, but you are ethically bound to contribute your fair share. Even as your grade is affected by the performance of others, their grades are dependent on you. If you have special circumstances, such as illness or a demanding work schedule, let the other members know right away. Try to find a way to do your part. It is neither professional nor honorable to accept a grade for work that you haven't done.

Effective speaking is a great asset on the job, in school and in your personal life. Knowing how to express yourself in an interview will help you get the job you want! And good communication skills at work will help you to perform well and avoid stress.

In college, you'll be asked to make oral presentations in class. At work, depending on your job, you'll present data and strategies verbally to groups. Effective interpersonal communications help to establish good relationships and address conflict in a positive way, in both your personal and professional lives.

Collaborating with Group Members

Successful collaboration requires teamwork. When collaborating in a small group, each member has a role to perform, and each member's full participation is required. The following is a list of typical group roles and responsibilities.

Before beginning a collaborative exercise, form a group and decide which member will perform the following roles and responsibilities. If you are collaborating with a partner, you can divide the responsibilities equally.

ROLES	RESPONSIBILITIES
Leader	The leader is responsible for interpreting the exercise directions, keeping the discussion on target, and making sure that everyone participates.
Recorder	The recorder acts as the secretary by taking notes and summarizing the group's findings or recording answers after the group achieves consensus (agreement).
Researcher	The researcher consults the textbook, the instructor, or other resources as needed to settle matters of confusion or controversy.
Reciter	The reciter reports back to the class, using the recorder's notes for reference.

Some collaborative activities may require different roles and responsibilities other than those described here. For example, if you are given a time limit for completing a task, someone must act as timekeeper. This could be a separate role, or it may be another responsibility added to the leader's or recorder's tasks. For groups that are larger or smaller than four members, new roles or new divisions of responsibilities can be created.

SUMMARY

Succeeding in the classroom means employing a wide range of techniques. Reading, writing, and effective note-taking are all essential to your success in college. Several *note-taking tips* are described in this chapter; using them to study will increase your understanding of the material, which in turn will boost your confidence and participation in class. *Classroom participation* and *collaborative learning* involve more than just discussion; being successful at group work will improve the quality of your group's project or presentation. It is also very important for you to understand the idea of being part of a group and working on projects with other people. This is a skill that will benefit you not only in college, but beyond.

Chapter 11

Outside the Classroom

LEARNING OBJECTIVES

By the end of this chapter you should be able to:

Prepare for class

Explain study strategies

Explain plagiarism and referencing

Think critically

What you learn in the classroom doesn't guarantee success in and of itself. So, as a student, your responsibility is to use your time out of class wisely. How to apply what you learn in class in order to be successful was discussed in the previous chapter. Refer to the chapter on Learning Styles for assistance in developing a study plan. The recommended study ratio for college courses is at least 2 hours out of class for every hour in class. So, look at it this way, if you are taking 12 hours, and you need to study 3 hours (on average) for each class, that's 36 hours a week. School is and should be your full-time job.

Marking Your Textbook

Once you have learned to identify the main idea, search out details and look for the author's conclusion. You can use those skills to highlight important points in the textbook and to make margin notes for review. What should you highlight? Concentrate on:

• Identifying the main idea and important supporting details

- Defining key terms
- Memorizing significant names and dates
- Answer the "Big 6" from your reading: Who? What? When? Where? Why? and How?

MAKING SENSE OF A PARAGRAPH

TCC students, especially new ones, often take a college reading course to develop their comprehension skills via vocabulary and textbook exercises. This book won't cover that material, but it will discuss paragraph structure, since most textbooks and other reading assignments are constructed in a series of paragraphs.

The typical paragraph contains a topic sentence stating the author's major point, the body of the paragraph consisting of one or more sentences providing supporting detail, and the conclusion which restates the main idea or serves as a transition to the next paragraph.

THE SQ3R SYSTEM

The *SQ3R study system* is widely used. While time consuming, it forces you to be very involved with the text. If you have difficulty reading and understanding even 10 pages of a text at one time, this system of reading can be particularly helpful. The five steps below are comprehensive but easy to remember.

S = *Survey* your reading assignments to get a general overview of the topic. What looks familiar? Has the instructor covered this in class? Pay particular attention if the author has used an introduction or list of objectives to be covered in a given chapter. Look at discussion or study questions and at the summary at the chapter's end. These will help you focus on what the author considers important.

Q = *Question*. Turn the chapter and unit headings into questions, and then read to answer the questions. Use the "Big 6" mentioned earlier—Who? What? When? Where? Why? and How?—to formulate your questions. Write your questions down as you survey the chapter. After reading each section, see how readily you can answer them.

R1 = *Read* to answer the questions you've developed. Find one or more main ideas and supporting details. Make margin notes. Pay attention to graphs, charts, and illustrations as you read. If you have the time, fold your paper in half vertically and put the questions on one side and the answers on the other. In this way, you can quickly review as needed. If you know you won't take the time to write out the questions and answers, concentrate on jotting down your questions as margin notes and highlight the material that answers them.

R2 = *Recall or recite*. Reciting material aloud to yourself helps you absorb the information. This step is especially helpful with definitions, date-and-event pairings, and materials that require memorization. It's also helpful to pause every 5–10 minutes (or after every section of text) and try to recall what you've already covered by reciting aloud or by jotting down the main ideas.

R3 = *Review, review, review!* Every review session helps you to retain the information for an upcoming test. Make sure your test review includes rereading your highlighted text and classroom notes.

Use the SQ3R study system on a reading assignment for one of your classes (you can use this class or another course). Survey the chapter and turn the chapter headings into questions. Then write your responses to the following:

Name of course

———————————————————————————————————————

———————————————————————————————————————

Name of textbook

———————————————————————————————————————

———————————————————————————————————————

Name of chapter

———————————————————————————————————————

———————————————————————————————————————

What are you expected to learn in this chapter? How do you know?

———————————————————————————————————————

———————————————————————————————————————

———————————————————————————————————————

What new terms or vocabulary words are in this chapter?

———————————————————————————————————————

———————————————————————————————————————

Take each heading and major subheading in the chapter and write a question that will be answered in that section of text.

_____

_____

_____

_____

_____

_____

STUDY SYSTEMS

There are many study systems you can use to better organize your information while studying for any class. *Charting* allows you to compare and contrast multiple topics, events, or people in relation to specific criteria or questions. *Concept* or *information maps* are visual guides to topics that may not be sequential by breaking them down from general to specific ideas. *Timelines* are used to organize material chronologically. *Process diagrams* show the methods, steps, and stages that describe how events occur. And *branching diagrams* start with a main idea and show how others branch off from it and then from one another. These are widely used by visual learners.

PLAGIARISM AND REFERENCING

Writing is a major requirement in most college courses and many universities now insist that all students demonstrate a mastery of basic writing skills before they can graduate. This may mean taking a specific sequence of writing courses or passing a test. Bottom line: You will write papers in almost every course you take. Some instructors will reduce your grade if a paper is poorly written from a technical perspective. If you don't use proper sentence structure, punctuation, and spelling, your grade may be dropped significantly. While you will, naturally, focus much of your attention on the content of papers you write, this cannot be the sole consideration. To succeed in college, you must learn to write clearly, concisely, and correctly.

Tallahassee Community College uses three types of documentation styles. These will help you avoid plagiarism. *Plagiarism* is defined in most dictionaries as the act of stealing intellectual property and asserting it to be your own. The property may be ideas, words, sentences, or concepts. To submit a paper that is not truly the product of your own mind and skill is to commit plagiarism. Avoid plagiarizing by showing where you found the material in such a way that someone who reads your paper can find the source, too. This is called documenting, referencing, or citing your sources.

The three types of documentation styles accepted at TCC are the **Modern Language Association style** (MLA), the **American Psychological Association Style** (APA), and the **Turabian Style**, which is also called Chicago Style. A documentation style manual will provide you with the correct technical information to write a strong paper. Different

Plagiarize \-rized; -rizing [plagiary]: to steal and pass off (the ideas or words of another) as one's own : use (a created production) without crediting the source : to commit literary theft : present as new and original an idea or product derived from an existing source - - plagiarizer *Merriam Webster's Collegiate Dictionary, 10th edition, 1994.*

TCC Student Handbook

- **Conduct Code, Article I, section Q.** The term "plagiarism" includes, but is not limited to, the use, by paraphrase or direct quotation, of the published or unpublished work of another person without full and clear acknowledgment. It also includes the unacknowledged use of materials prepared by another person or agency engaged in the selling of term papers or other academic materials.

- **Article IV, Proscribed Conduct: Section B: Conduct—Rules and Regulations.** Any student found to have committed the following misconduct is subject to the disciplinary sanctions outlined in Article IV:1: Acts of dishonesty, including but not limited to the following: Cheating, **plagiarism**, or other forms of academic dishonesty . . .

FAQ's about Writing Research Papers

Question 8: *My professor keeps talking about plagiarism. What does she mean? Can you get kicked out of school for plagiarism?* Your professor is referring to situations in which students put information into their papers but fail to acknowledge the source of the information. It is like stealing the information. Sometimes **plagiarism** occurs out of ignorance when students misunderstand the concept of paraphrase, thinking they do not have to cite the source if they transform the author's into their own words. On the other hand, sometimes students intentionally take material from sources and pass it off as their own. Some professors try to distinguish between these two situations; others don't. The TCC Student Handbook clearly defines the consequences for plagiarism, and, yes, it is possible to be dismissed from school for plagiarism.

TCC English Department

"To submit to an instructor a paper that is not truly the product of your own mind and skill is to commit **plagiarism**. Bluntly put, plagiarism is the act of stealing ideas and/or the words of another and presenting them as your own. It is a form of cheating and a kind of academic dishonesty which can incur severe penalties. Accurate and honest quotation and documentation is the mark of a good writer. Professional writers always give credit where credit is due."

Citation guides and sample research papers following APA, MLA, and Turabian guidelines are available. See the TCC website at Student Library Guide for websites that offer further information on proper citing and the good and bad of paraphrasing.

courses require different documentation styles. MLA style is the most widely-used format in general education courses and is preferred in most English and humanities courses. The APA style is used in business and psychology courses and is the most commonly used style in social and natural sciences courses. The Chicago style is used in history and religion courses. It is important to remember that, for any paper requiring documentation, you should first ask your instructor which style to use.

CRITICAL THINKING

Your college experience will help you to develop critical and creative thinking skills. Critical thinking means analyzing data and solving problems. Creative thinking helps you find new approaches to problems in your personal and professional lives.

Critical thinking is a process of identifying different views, questioning each one, seeking additional information, and then constructing meaning to arrive at a conclusion.

Alternative Views

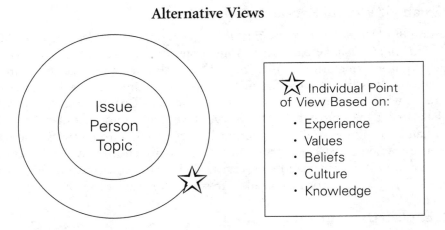

From **College and Career Success,** *2nd edition by Marsha Fralick. Copyright © by Kendall/Hunt Publishing Company. Reprinted by permission*

What Are Some Tips for Critical Thinking?

1. Be aware of your mindset. A mindset is a pattern of thought that you use out of habit. You develop patterns of thinking based on your personal experiences, culture, and environment. When the situation changes, your old mindset may need to change as well.

2. Be willing to say, "I don't know." With this attitude, you're open to exploring new ideas. In today's rapidly changing world, it is not possible to know everything. Rather than trying to know everything, it is more important to be able to find the information you need.

3. Practice tolerance for other people's ideas. We all have a different view of the world based on our own experiences and can benefit from an open exchange of information.

4. Try to look for several answers and understand many points of view. The world is not either-or or black-and-white. Looking at all the possibilities is the first step in finding a creative solution.

5. Understand before criticizing. Life is not about justifying your point of view. It's important to understand first, then offer your suggestions.

6. Realize that your emotions can impede your clear thinking. We all have beliefs that we value and when someone questions them it's difficult to listen to a different point of view. Open your mind to see all the alternatives then construct your reasonable view.

7. Note the source of the information you're analyzing. Political announcements are required to include information about the person or organization paying for the ad. Knowing who paid for an advertisement can help you understand and evaluate the point of view being promoted.

8. Ask the question, "What makes the author think so?" In this way, you can discover what premises the author is using to justify his or her position.

A critical thinking exercise is below. The object of the maze is to find out how to get to the center. Give it a try!

SUMMARY

This chapter has been all about how to get more from what you learn in class. The *SQ3R* study system, though time consuming, will help you tremendously. So, too, will the understanding that doing work outside the classroom is a necessary part of learning. Make sure to take notes, study, and spend time on subject matter for your own understanding, not just because the instructor assigns homework. *Plagiarism* is considered academic dishonesty—a very serious offense and is to be avoided. It's essential to give appropriate credit when using resources to write academic papers and other works. You can use the *APA, MLA, or Turabian* documentation formats to *cite your sources*. **Critical thinking** is also an important aspect to learning outside the classroom. Be sure that you are reading the material actively, searching for meaning and purpose within it, and using all your resources to truly learn not only in the classroom, but beyond.

Chapter 12

Test Taking and Test Anxiety: Don't Sweat It!

LEARNING OBJECTIVES

By the end of this chapter, you should be able to:

Identify and list the types of assessment given in college

Understand how to prepare and take subjective and objective tests

Develop a testing routine

Define text anxiety

Identify characteristics, symptoms and causes of test anxiety

Develop strategies to reduce test anxiety before, during and after a test

DEVELOPING TEST TAKING SKILLS

Being a skilled test-taker is absolutely essential to college success, but these skills don't come naturally to everyone. Therefore, it's important to know how tests are created in order to know how and what to study.

Tests are created in many ways. **Instructor-generated tests** are drawn from the instructor's own question bank; typically, these test questions come from material presented in class. Instructors can also use **publisher-generated tests**, from a test bank supplied by the textbook publisher; the questions on these tests focus mostly on material from the book. Students are responsible for all material on the test, whether it has been covered in class or not. Some instructors do **"mix and match" tests**, which contain a combination of any or all of the following: textbook information, lecture material, outside readings, videos and class discussion. A **lab quiz** could require recognition of slides or demonstrations performed or created during lab class. Music and/or art quizzes frequently incorporate material learned outside class.

CONSIDER THE FOLLOWING STUDENT

Has this Ever Happened to You?

Janice has a midterm in her math class today, and she feels sick just thinking about it. She spent the entire night cramming, hoping it would finally make sense. She has always had trouble with math and avoids it like the plague. Instead of working harder or asking for help, she puts off studying until the night before. She knows she has to pass because she wants to be a doctor, and it's a required course. Her parents will be very disappointed if she doesn't do well. Somehow, she has to pull off a miracle.

Feeling tired and too nauseous to eat, Janice grabs some coffee on the way to school. Traffic is heavy, and her midterm starts soon. Will she make it in time? Her palms feel sweaty. Her head hurts. She tries to take some deep breaths, but it doesn't help. If she can't pass this test, she must be really dumb! All her friends have passed this class, and they say it's easy. Why is it so hard for her?

When she gets to school, the parking lot is full. Her panic increases as she hunts for a spot. By the time she finds one, far from her building, the exam is in five minutes and the class is all the way across campus. She sprints across the courtyard, hoping she brought her calculator and pencil. She arrives two minutes late; the instructor gives her an annoyed look.

Janice finds a seat, her heart beating practically outside her chest. She catches her breath and scans the test. It looks really hard. She starts shaking, and her pencil drops from her hand, which is even sweatier now. Suddenly, the text looks like gibberish, and everything she studied the night before is gone from her head. She looks around. Everyone else is flying through the test. What's wrong with her? Why can't she do this? Janice stares at the test until the instructor calls time. She has only made a few incoherent scribbles on the paper. She gets up and turns it in, feeling utterly miserable.

Discussion Questions

Get into groups of three to four. Assign one person to be the Recorder, who will write down everything the group discusses, and assign another person to be the Speaker, who will present the group's ideas to the class. Discuss the following questions with your group, referring to specific portions of the scenario above:

- What are some of the issues facing Janice?
- What could she have done differently before and during the test to resolve these issues?
- What should she do now that she has failed the test to make sure it doesn't happen again?

Be ready to share your ideas with your class.

Types of Assessments

Before discussing how to prepare for tests, quizzes and exams, let's define them. Generally, the *amount* of material covered dictates the type of evaluative tool. A **quiz** covers a class to a week's worth of material, depending on the instructor. A **test** usually covers a chapter to several weeks' worth of material. An **exam** refers to the midterm and final examinations; each can cover several tests' worth of material. Some instructors use the words "test" and "exam" interchangeably, so it's important to know what your instructor means. It is always important to check the actual weight of the quiz, test or exam toward your final grade.

Testing is an age-old method to find out what students know about assigned course material and/or how well they've mastered a skill or concept. Exams force students to learn the material. They also give instructors valuable feedback on how well they have taught the material and whether they need to modify their content or approach. Exams also give feedback to students on how well they understand and can apply what they've learned. This assessment should tell students whether they need to modify their method of studying.

Types of Questions You Will See

There are two general types of exam questions you'll encounter in college. They are Objective and Subjective questions. Most exams mix the two.

Objective Questions

Multiple-choice, matching, true-false and fill-in-the-blank questions are considered "objective" questions. This means they usually have one specific answer, with little variation in the acceptable response. Tips for taking exams with objective questions are listed below. Of course, none of these suggestions are more important that solid preparation, but once you've done all you can to prepare for an exam, a certain "testwise-ness" is valuable.

Preparing for Objective Question Exams

1. MAJOR TOPICS. Make a list of major topics in the course or unit. Skim assignment sheets, lecture notes, outlines of outside reading and quiz papers so to be sure the list is complete.

2. SUMMARY. Write a summary or outline of related material for each of the major topics. Place particular emphasis on relationships among the topics.

3. SYSTEMATIC REVIEW. Go over the material step by step. Apply the most time to the topics you most need to review.

4. MOCK EXAM. Make a list of probable questions. Include what you know about your instructor's interests and points of emphasis. Once you've gone over all the material, a mock exam is an excellent way to review. It puts you in a simulated test situation to give you important practice for the real exam.

DEVELOP A TEST ROUTINE

- Arrive on time.

- Jot down cues.

- Survey the test.

- READ ALL DIRECTIONS.

- Answer easy questions first.

- Skip and return to difficult questions.

- Make an educated guess for Multiple Choices and Matching.

- Never leave an answer blank.

- Use all your allotted time.

- Check your work before handing in your test.

5.   REST. Adequate sleep and rest are essential! It's impossible to think clearly after cramming all night, and many students who do find themselves unable to recall the very material they'd grasped just hours before. An early bedtime, if at all possible, boosts your test performance.

6.   RELAX! Many students face every exam with such emotion that they can't demonstrate their true knowledge. If anxiety interferes with your ability to perform on a test, then avoid comparing notes with your classmates just before one. And remember: during exam week, comparing notes *after* a final may give you a feeling of failure before you take the next one.

Tips for Taking Exams with Objective Questions

1.   When you take an exam, be absolutely certain what is expected. Pay very close attention the entire time. Listen to all directions and read all written instructions as carefully as possible. Ask questions if necessary. Is there a penalty for guessing? Do incorrect answers count more against your grade than correct answers do toward it?

2.   Find out exactly how much time you have and estimate the amount of time per question (or per five questions) that you can afford to spend.

3.   While exams with objective questions often don't allow enough time to read the entire document twice before starting, at least glance through it for sections that might be more time-consuming than others. Plan accordingly.

4.   Put off answering the more difficult items. Mark the ones you skip in the margin. Don't get stuck and not finish the exam! And remember to return to the unfinished items before you turn in your exam; allow extra time for this.

5.   On multiple-choice questions, read all four or five choices before answering, even if you know the first or second is correct. Otherwise, should the last item be "None of the Above," "All of the Above," or "Two of the Above," you may have misunderstood the question and thus the answer.

6.   If there are five choices for a multiple-choice question, read each and cross out the ones you know to be wrong. When in doubt, this narrows the field, and you stand a better chance of guessing correctly among two or three answers than among five.

7.   Remember, almost everyone misses questions. If you can avoid getting jittery when you do, and go on with confidence, you'll come out on top. Don't blow the exam because you think you missed too many items.

8.   Don't panic if you see someone moving along faster than you. If someone leaves early, he or she may have given up. Besides, exams are often constructed to last longer than the time given.

9.   After you leave the examination room, debrief yourself. Jot down the topics covered in the exam, noting the sections of your textbook(s) covered. Note the strengths and weaknesses of your exam preparation.

10. Plan ahead to do better next time, especially by eliminating the mistakes that have caused you some trouble.

Subjective Questions

In contrast to an objective question, for which there is one specific answer, subjective questions may have several correct responses. Short answer and essay questions are examples, often more difficult to answer since there is no one correct response.

Essay Questions

Essay questions are designed to reveal your ability to make and support valid generalizations, or to apply broad principles to specific instances. The question will be directed toward some major area of thought. For example, in a literature course, you might be asked to contrast two authors' opinions about the nature of humanity.

Preparing for Exams with Essay Questions

1. Preparation for an essay exam, as for any exam, requires close and careful rereading and review of text and lecture notes. With this kind of exam, the emphasis is on the major concepts covered in the unit.

2. Find out what exam format the instructor will use, whether a series of short answer questions, one long essay, etc. Ask him or her which format to expect. This differs from asking what specific questions will be on the exam. In fact, many instructors announce in advance the general areas the exam will cover—concepts, issues, controversies, theories, rival interpretations, etc.

3. Review your lecture notes for concepts that have been central to class discussion. Begin by asking yourself about the main ideas and relationships in the material. Review your notes broadly; don't worry about detail at first. Review the major headings and chapter summaries in your text. Boil the material down to a tight outline form.

4. Once you organize the main concepts in a logical pattern, fill in the details. On an essay exam, you'll face the task of arriving at a sound generalization, then proving it through skillful use of detail. You must, therefore, have these details at your command. Remember: no one detail is crucial. Select those that best prove or support a concept.

5. Some students profit by making up sample questions, then practicing their answers. In a history course, for instance, you might test yourself by answering questions such as, "Explain what John C. Calhoun meant by the term *concurrent majority* and compare his ideas to Jefferson's on majority rule." However, devoting *too* much time to specific questions could throw you off if those aren't the ones on the exam!

6. Part of the groundwork for every exam is mastering the terminology used in the course. Getting this done early is crucial to understanding the material and preparing adequately.

Tips for Taking Exams with Essay Questions

1. When you get the exam, look for the point value of each question. If the questions aren't weighted equally, decide how much time to spend on each. Allow more time for longer questions and their answers. If necessary, borrow time from the short

answers. If the point value isn't listed, ask your instructor whether all the questions have an equal value and, if not, what the values are for each.

2. First, read the directions carefully and glance over all the questions. Then read each question carefully before answering. Try to understand exactly what is being asked. An essay question always has a controlling idea expressed in one or two words. Find the key words and underline them.

3. As you skim the test, jot down key words or phrases for each question. This will serve to stimulate other ideas. Make the initial sentence of your answer the best possible one-sentence response. Elaborate in subsequent sentences. As ideas about other questions occur to you, immediately jot them down on scratch paper before they slip away.

WHAT EXACTLY IS TEST ANXIETY?

It's common to feel some nervousness or apprehension before, during or after an exam. This type of anxiety can be a powerful motivation for you to prepare thoroughly, seek help with confusing concepts, and focus and perform during the exam. However, some students experience anxiety to such a degree that it weakens their performances and interferes with their learning. This is what experts refer to as **test anxiety**. These students have difficulty demonstrating what they really do know during a test because of overwhelming feelings of nervousness and lack of control.

Test anxiety is *not* the same as doing poorly on a test because your mind is on personal or financial concerns. These can also impede your concentration and performance, but are considered "normal" distractions that everyone has from time to time. Test anxiety is an ongoing problem that occurs in almost every testing situation for a particular student. Sometimes it occurs only on specific types of tests, such as essay or multiple-choice, or during tests on specific subjects, such as math or history. In those cases, the student doesn't have test anxiety while being tested in other subjects, but has mild to severe symptoms when tested in a particular subject.

Performance Anxiety

Test anxiety is actually a type of **performance anxiety**, a feeling one might have in situations that carry great pressure to succeed. You could experience performance anxiety while trying out for a play, speaking before an audience, stepping onto the platform at a diving meet, or going to an important job interview.

Characteristics of Anxiety

Anxiety is a natural human response to a threatening situation. It's a form of the **"fight-or-flight" response**, in which the mind and body become alert to an attack or the need to escape from a threat. Performance anxieties, and test anxieties in particular, are specific responses to **evaluative situations**. That means a person is being observed or evaluated by others. The "threat" in these situations is the possibility of failure and loss of self-esteem due to criticism or low scores. Depending on the intensity of one's anxiety, its emotional, behavioral and cognitive aspects can hinder the ability to perform.

Test or performance anxiety typically occurs:

- in the presence of a difficult, threatening or challenging situation,
- when a person believes he or she is inadequate or incapable of meeting the challenge, and
- when he or she fears the consequences of possible failure.

Anxiety and Arousal

To perform well in a challenging situation, you must be psychologically and physically alert. You can't do well on an exam if you're nearly asleep! This level of psychological and physical "alertness" is called **arousal**. Some degree of arousal is needed for your best performance. Increasing arousal is often called "psyching up"; you prepare to take on a challenge. Anxiety occurs when the intensity of arousal becomes so great that you begin to feel nervous and tense. Then the anxiety becomes a distraction, and your performance declines. Some people get "psyched out." *For your best performance, you need to get "psyched up" but not "psyched out."*

What Is the Optimal Level of Arousal?

How do you know when you're aroused enough to do well on an exam but not so much that it will cause debilitating anxiety? If you're properly psyched up, you'll be able to focus and your performance will feel natural. If you're psyched out and your anxiety has taken over, you may experience:

- distracting thoughts of failure
- an inability to pick out important environmental cues
- becoming distracted by irrelevant environmental cues
- interpreting the results of physical arousal, such as muscle tension, increased heart rate and respiration, as signs of fear
- excessive muscle tension
- an attempt to avoid or escape the situation
- giving up

Symptoms of Test Anxiety

Most of the effects of test anxiety occur while taking the exam. The most common symptom is to freeze up and forget everything you studied. This is called a **mental block**. Perhaps you start reading the questions and, suddenly, they don't make sense. They may even seem like a different language. A less severe example: having to reread questions several times to understand them.

Another common symptom of test anxiety is panic. For instance, you might find you don't know the answer to even one question, or that you can't finish the exam in the allotted time. You may also worry about your performance compared to that of others, which is more likely in competitive class situations. Perhaps you look around at other test takers and think they're doing well, even finishing early, thereby increasing your level of panic. Or you may find you're easily distracted during the exam.

> ## DID YOU KNOW?
>
> If you experience test or performance anxiety, you're not alone. Approximately 20 percent of U.S. college students experience test anxiety, and most athletes, actors and artists report experiencing some form of performance anxiety during their careers.

Some even plot ways to escape from a test, such as sneaking out the back door or faking an illness. This is the "flight" option of the "fight-or-flight" response.

You may also experience test anxiety before an exam, while studying for or even walking to it. You might forget information already learned or have difficulty concentrating. Physical discomfort—such as nausea, rapid pulse, excessive perspiration and muscle tension—is also symptomatic. You can exhaust yourself by worrying so much. Some find they no longer care about doing well by the time the test arrives because they're so drained.

Test anxiety symptoms can be divided into categories as follows:

Physical symptoms can include headaches, nausea, diarrhea, extreme body temperature changes, shortness of breath, light-headedness or fainting, muscle tension, perspiration, rapid heartbeat and dry mouth.

Emotional symptoms can include excessive feelings of fear, disappointment, anger, depression, uncontrollable crying or laughing, and feelings of helplessness.

Behavioral symptoms can include fidgeting, pacing, substance abuse and avoidance of things associated with a testing situation. They can also include inability to act, make decisions, express yourself or deal with everyday situations. These symptoms may cause you to have difficulty reading and understanding questions, organizing your thoughts, or retrieving key words and concepts.

Psychological symptoms can include feelings of apprehension, uneasiness, upset and self-doubt.

Cognitive symptoms can include racing thoughts, a mental block, difficulty concentrating, negative self-talk, feelings of dread, comparing yourself to others, and difficulty organizing your thoughts.

Causes of Test Anxiety

What causes test anxiety? Why do some experience it so much more than others? Can a person prevent the causes of test anxiety before it becomes a problem?

Test anxiety can develop for a number of reasons, including the following:

- **Lack of preparation** or inadequate preparation is the main cause of test anxiety. When students cram at the last minute due to procrastination, they feel less confident about the material than those who follow a structured study plan. Poor time management, poor study habits and a lack of organization can cause some students to feel completely overwhelmed. Rather, anticipate what the exam will cover. Know you've studied as well as possible. Thus you'll enter the test situation with a more positive attitude, confident you're in control. The more you practice *knowing* the material, the more you *will* know the material. If it's all learned at the last minute, you just can't know it as well!

- **Prior negative testing experiences** can activate anxiety over an upcoming test. Students who have blanked out on tests or been unable to perform well in testing situations can develop **anticipatory anxiety**. Worrying about how anxiety will affect you can be as debilitating as the anxiety itself. What's more, your anxiety can build as the testing situation approaches, interfering with your ability to prepare. By forcing yourself to "forget" those past experiences and view this new test as a separate event or an opportunity to do your best, you can focus on your current studies without the past creeping in.

- **Negative thought processes**, including lack of confidence and fear of failure, may also contribute to test anxiety. The pressure to perform well on exams is a great motivator—unless it becomes so extreme as to be irrational. Perfectionism and feelings of unworthiness create unreasonable goals for testing situations. When a student's self-esteem is too closely tied to the outcome of any one test, the results can be devastating. Indeed, some students spend more time focused on the consequences of failure than on preparing to succeed.

- **Expectations.** Your perceptions of others' expectations for you may be inaccurate. If you worry that you'll alienate people you love unless you do well in college, you may become fearful and anxious that you'll disappoint or anger them. If you think you can't live up to their expectations, tests may make you especially anxious.

  Suppose your parents become angry if you earn a grade lower than A or B. Talk it over with them to determine the source of their anger. Perhaps they think a C or below means you aren't trying enough or aren't committed to getting an education—even when they've made a financial sacrifice to give you the chance. However, there may be other reasons why you're not performing as expected in a course. You may have been unprepared for the difficulty of the course. Maybe illness or other hardships have affected your performance. It's unreasonable to expect you to achieve someone else's ideal grade, but not unreasonable to expect you to do your best. If a C represents your best effort, then it's a good grade. Try to separate yourself from others' expectations of you. Focus instead on what you expect from yourself and work hard to achieve it.

- **Grades and self-esteem.** Test anxiety often results from placing too great an emphasis on grades. A low grade, for some, means, "I don't measure up." The result is a loss of self-esteem. One way to reduce test anxiety is to emphasize *performance* instead of grades. Rather than letting grades control your feelings, take control of your academic performance.

  Turn each testing situation into an opportunity for self-assessment. Use tests to track your performance in a course. Keep a record of the number and types of items you missed, those you now need to review, your anxiety during the test, and your level of preparation. Over time, you may see a pattern in your study and testing behaviors. For example, if you consistently miss the same type of question, or if your anxiety goes up when you haven't prepared well, you'll know what and how much to study for the next test.

  When you emphasize performance over grades, a test becomes a personal challenge. It offers a chance to apply your knowledge to new problems and tasks. It offers the opportunity to discover your strengths and weaknesses. Improved performance is the goal. Grades are not a measure of self-worth. They are just a way to keep score.

- **Feelings of helplessness.** Are you self-motivated (internal locus of control) or other-motivated (external locus of control)? Other-motivated students often don't see a connection between studying and grades. They blame poor grades on the perceived unfairness of their instructor or the difficulty of the test rather than their own lack of preparation. As a result, they feel helpless and out of control, thus experiencing test anxiety. The more self-motivated you are, however, the more likely you'll see a connection between preparation and grades. When you're well prepared for a test, you're in control of your emotions and reactions. You'll enter the classroom feeling calm and confident, ready to do your best.

Everyone has a unique personality and set of experiences that can contribute to test anxiety, which is why people differ so much in their levels of anxiety during a test. If you're prone to high levels of test anxiety, accept it and deal with it, using the strategies suggested below. Don't feel badly about yourself because you suffer from test anxiety; instead, focus on what you can do to change it.

STRATEGIES TO REDUCE TEST ANXIETY
Before the Test

- **Preparation.** If you practice and study enough, you can approach any test with confidence. Your responses may even become automatic when you're well prepared. In other words, thorough preparation leads to a performance much less affected by anxiety. To accomplish this, build good study habits and spread your major exam review over several days. When preparing for exam week, study 15–20 minutes per day per subject, so that the material isn't new to you and you don't feel overwhelmed. Naturally, you should attend class regularly, complete all assignments well and on time, and make and take practice tests to prepare for real ones. To be sure you've covered everything, you may also wish to make a list of items to study. As you check them off your list, your confidence will grow; you've mastered each. Even so, you should still review these items along with newer material to ensure that you retain them.

- **Keep a positive attitude.** Develop reasonable expectations of how you'll perform on a test. And don't allow your grade to depend on just one exam! Instead, complete all your assignments well and on time. That way, your grade won't hinge on the upcoming exam. Avoid negative and irrational thoughts about catastrophic results. Be sure to reward yourself for meeting your study objectives and performing well on tests.

- **Relaxation techniques.** If you start to feel anxious while preparing for the test, you can do:

  - **Deep breathing exercises:** Hold your breath for ten seconds, and then slowly release it. Repeat until you feel your anxiety and tension decrease.

  - **Visualization:** Picture yourself taking the test, feeling calm and confident. Imagine you've prepared enough so that the answers come easily. See yourself getting a good grade. Know that you did your best.

  - **Muscle relaxation:** Clench different muscle groups for a few seconds, then release them; this will relieve the tension you're feeling. Perhaps a hot shower or bath will further relax your muscles. Consider a healthy workout at the gym, a long walk or simple stretching exercises. Combine these muscle relaxation techniques with deep breathing for maximum effect.

  - **Clearing your mind:** Find an activity to distract you for a short time, such as talking to a friend, watching TV or eating a good meal. Just don't clear your mind so often that you have no time to prepare for the test!

- **Learn good test-taking skills.** Develop a plan for taking your test. Once you receive it, survey it. What types of questions are there? Next, do a "memory dump," writing all the material you've memorized on the back of your test. You won't have to keep it in your head and run the risk of losing it later from nerves.

  Now, answer the questions you know right off. This will give you confidence that you've done at least *some* of the test well. If you get stuck on a question, move on to something else and come back later. To answer an essay question, make an outline and use it as a guide. Remember: read the directions thoroughly before you begin the test. Read each question and plan your time so that you have enough for each. If you have extra time, go back and check your work.

- **Be healthy.** When you're physically and emotionally exhausted, your body and mind aren't as able to handle anxiety and stress. Thus, you can improve your resistance to anxiety by getting enough rest, eating properly and taking care of your physical health. The night before an exam, you should get 7–8 hours of sleep. You'll perform much better than if you cram all night.

  If you can't find time to be healthy, consider seeking assistance with your time management skills.

  Don't go to the exam on an empty stomach! Fresh fruits and vegetables are recommended to reduce stress. Avoid caffeine, which can make you jumpy. Stay away from processed foods, artificial sweeteners, carbonated soft drinks, chocolate, eggs, fried food, junk food, pork, red meat, sugar, white flour, chips, foods containing preservatives and those with heavy spices. These foods have been shown to cause stress, and that's the last thing you need more of during your exam!

- **Practice the performance.** Time limits on an exam, a tied score, and the audience at your performance are all stimuli that can increase your arousal and thus add to your anxiety. If you practice under test-like conditions, however, you'll become less sensitive to these stimuli.

To prepare for an exam, work through a practice test or two with the same time constraints that you'll face on the real one. Don't look at your notes during this; simulate as many conditions of the actual exam as possible. For an athletic or artistic performance, practice with distractions or with an audience. For conditions that you can't reproduce, create them in your mind. Visualization is a powerful tool; it can calm you.

- **Approach the exam with confidence.** Use the strategies listed above to walk into your exam with confidence. View the test as an opportunity to show how much you've studied and to be rewarded for it.

During the Test

- **Regulate your arousal level.** In cases of anxiety, the goal is to lower your arousal, so that you feel psyched up but not psyched out. Some effective ways involve regulating physical responses like rapid breathing and muscle tension.

  - **Deep breathing:** When anxious, we often take shallow breaths. We feel we're not getting enough air, which in turn makes us *more* anxious. This vicious cycle is interrupted by breathing slowly and deeply. Your mind and body begin to relax.

    To learn to breathe deeply, place a hand on your stomach and inhale, making your abdomen expand. As you exhale, your abdomen should move inward. Practice taking 10–15 slow deep breaths in a row, 2–3 times per day, training your body to breathe deeply and relax. Then, during a stressful situation such as taking a test, take 2–3 deep breaths, and your body will relax.

  - **Progressive muscle relaxation:** We also tense our muscles when anxious, so add muscle relaxation to your deep breathing in a stressful situation, such as taking a test. Focus on a particular muscle group (e.g., shoulders) and alternate tensing and relaxing them. Next, focus on releasing tension by saying the word "relax" over and over in your mind. By consciously relaxing your muscles, you'll relax your mind as well.

  - **Reduce distractions:** Distractions are additional stimuli that increase arousal. Explore ways to reduce distractions in your immediate environment. Sit away from others, perhaps in a far corner of the room. Wear comfortable clothing, preferably in layers so that you can put something on if you're cold or take something off if you're warm. If the person sitting next to you is distracting, negative or agitated, move away. Try not to sit near a window. Be sure to turn off your cell phone, as it will distract you and possibly others.

ALWAYS REMEMBER . . .

Give yourself plenty of time on test day to arrive and get situated beforehand. Avoid rushing, which can make you anxious. Avoid talking to others about the test, which can rattle you and make you doubt your preparation and understanding. Don't arrive too early, however, if this makes you anxious as well.

· **Practice test-taking rituals:** Rituals are repetitive behaviors that give us a sense of familiarity and help us focus, thus reducing anxiety. A basketball player who bounces the ball three times before each free-throw has a ritual. The singer who carries a rabbit's foot to each performance has a ritual. You may already have some rituals, such as getting a drink of water before an exam or using a particular pencil or pen. Just a note of caution: select rituals that aren't harmful or distracting to others, such as tapping your pencil on your desk four times before each question, which could annoy your classmates and hurt their performance.

• **Control the fear.** The underlying source of test or performance anxiety is the fear of failure. Pay attention to what you're thinking and saying to yourself in stressful situations. This **self-talk** will likely reflect an expectation or fear of failure. You can begin to control this fear or change the expectation by changing your self-talk.

· **Positive self-talk:** Purposely filling your mind with positive statements about your abilities can crowd out the negative self-talk. Even if you don't believe the positives, say them anyway: "I'm ready, I can do this!" Determine your most important positive messages by writing down your four most common negative thoughts. Then write down the opposite of each statement. Repeat the positives to yourself daily for at least two weeks, and again just before and during the test or performance.

· **On-task self-talk:** Counter distractions and help yourself focus on the task at hand. Talk yourself through the task step-by-step, telling yourself that you're succeeding! It won't help to think about past mistakes or future consequences, so put them out of your mind. Focus on what you must do; be your own cheerleader.

Figure 1	**DEVELOPING POSITIVE SELF-TALK**

Write down the most common negative thoughts you have during a testing situation.

1. _____

2. _____

3. _____

4. _____

Write down the opposite of each negative thought. These are your positive thoughts.

1. _____

2. _____

3. _____

4. _____

DEALING WITH TEST ANXIETY—A PRIMER

Preparing for or Anticipating Test Anxiety

- What is it you have to do? Focus on dealing with it.
- Just take one step at a time.
- Think about what you can do about it. That's better than getting anxious.
- No negative or panicky self-statements; just think rationally.
- Don't worry; it won't help anything.

Confronting and Handling Test Anxiety

- Don't think about fear; just think about what you must do.
- Relax; you're in control. Take slow, deep breaths.
- Expect some anxiety; it's a reminder not to panic but to relax and cope.
- Tenseness can be an ally, a friend, a coping mechanism.

Coping with the Feeling of Being Overwhelmed

- When the fear comes, just pause.
- Keep your focus on the present; what is it you have to do?
- You should expect your fear to increase somewhat.
- Don't try to eliminate fear totally; just keep it manageable.
- You can convince yourself to do it. You can reason your fear away.
- It's not the worst thing that can happen.
- Do something that will prevent your thinking about fear.
- Describe what's around you to avoid worrying.

Reinforcing Self-Statements

- It worked! You did it!
- It wasn't as bad as you expected.
- You made more out of the fear than it was worth.
- You're getting better. You're learning to cope more smoothly.
- You can be pleased with your progress.
- You like how you handled it. You can be proud of it.

· **Gain perspective:** Sometimes negative thoughts in stressful situations focus on potentially drastic consequences of failure. This behavior is called *catastrophizing*. In most cases, the imagined consequences are much more severe than the reality of the situation. Focusing on such then increases your anxiety and interferes with your performance.

It's important to recognize that one mistake doesn't equal failure and one bad performance doesn't mean you're worthless. Take time to evaluate the most likely consequences of your performance. If you find that you tend to catastrophize, develop some phrases that are more realistic and repeat them to yourself prior to and during the exam. An example would be to replace "If I fail this, my life will be over!" (catastrophizing statement) with "This is just one exam" (more realistic statement).

• **Engage in productive behavior.** During the test, follow these tips to reduce anxiety:

· Read the directions carefully.

· Budget your test-taking time.

· Change positions to help you relax.

· If you go blank, skip the question and move on. Don't focus on having skipped it. Circle the question so you'll remember to come back to it, then put it out of your mind and focus on the next question.

· If you're taking an essay test and you go blank on the whole test, pick one question and start writing an outline. It may trigger the answers in your mind.

· Don't panic when other students start handing in their tests. There's no reward for being the first one done. Take the time you need to do your best.

· Check your work carefully before turning in your test.

After the Test

• List what worked and maintain those strategies. It doesn't matter how minor they are; they're building blocks to success.

• List what didn't help to reduce your level of anxiety.

- Celebrate that you are on the road to overcoming this obstacle.
- Now, forget about the test. There's nothing you can do until it's graded and returned. Put your attention and effort on new assignments and tests.
- When the graded test is returned to you, analyze it to see how you could have done better. Learn from your mistakes and from what you did well. Apply this knowledge when you take your next test by coming up with a specific plan for how to improve.

SUMMARY

This chapter covers the **types of assessments** and questions you'll see on tests during your college career. It's vital to know how to prepare for and take both **subjective** and **objective** types of tests. The purpose of having a study and test routine is to be better prepared. Walking into an exam thoroughly prepared will reduce your test anxiety.

The chapter also defines **test anxiety** and discusses typical **characteristics**, **symptoms** and **causes** for this type of **performance anxiety**. Suggestions are given for reducing anxiety before, during and after a test. By following these tips, each time students with text anxiety take a test, they should feel less and less anxiety until it's not a disruptive issue.

MANAGING TEST ANXIETY
Awareness Check
Do You Suffer from Test Anxiety?

Complete the short evaluation below by reading each statement and considering your previous testing experience. You may want to consider all such experience or focus on one particular subject at a time, such as math, science or history. Indicate how often each statement describes you by choosing a number from one to five and writing it in each blank.

Never	Rarely	Sometimes	Often	Always
1	2	3	4	5

I have visible signs of nervousness, such as sweaty palms and shaky hands, right before a test.

I have "butterflies" in my stomach before a test.

I feel nauseated before a test.

I read through the test and feel that I don't know any of the answers.

I panic before and during a test.

My mind goes blank during a test.

I remember the information that I blanked on once I get out of the testing situation.

I have trouble sleeping the night before a test.

I make mistakes on easy questions or put answers in the wrong places.

I have difficulty choosing answers.

Scoring: Add up your score. It should range from 10 to 50. A low score (10–19) means that you don't suffer from test anxiety. In fact, if your score was extremely low (close to 10), a little more anxiety may help to keep you focused during an exam. Scores between 20 and 35 indicate that although you exhibit some of the characteristics of text anxiety, your level of stress and tension is probably healthy. Scores over 35 suggest that you are experiencing an unhealthy level of test anxiety.

Source: Nist and Diehl (1990)

WHAT WOULD YOU SUGGEST?

Fred suffers from many symptoms of test anxiety. Before and during any testing situation, he experiences many different thoughts and reactions. Help him come up with solutions to each symptom.

SYMPTOM	SOLUTION
He sweats profusely during the test.	
He feels muscle tension in his neck before and during the test.	
He feels helpless because he knows studying won't matter.	
He has trouble dealing with personal matters because he's so wrapped up thinking about his test.	
He feels very upset and uneasy, and doubts whether he should be in school.	
He finds it difficult to focus on anything before or during the test, because his mind is crammed with information and is constantly racing.	
During the test, he starts thinking of his peers and how well they must be doing, especially when they start flipping their pages and turning in their tests.	

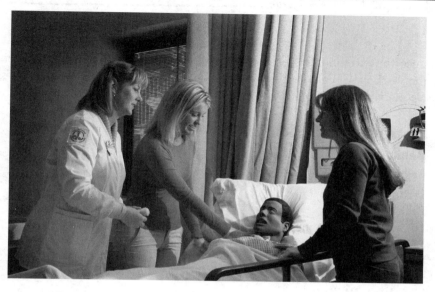

Chapter 13

After Graduation

LEARNING OBJECTIVES

By the end of this chapter, you should be able to

List and identify basic workplace skills

Identify workforce trends, including those reflecting your career goals

Identify skills and preparation for successful job interviews

Write effective résumés and cover letters

THE WORKFORCE

Once you've earned a degree or certificate, you'll most likely enter the workforce full time. The world of work is changing every day—and those changes will affect your career. You'll need to know which skills your prospective employer is seeking, what type of work environment you'll enter, the impact of technology on your future, and the benefits of lifelong learning.

Given today's rapid technological advances, current students may be preparing for jobs that don't even exist yet. After graduation, many will end up in jobs unrelated to their college majors—48% of them, according to one researcher. More important than your major, therefore, are the basic skills to equip you for future success.

According to the U.S. Department of Labor, the following skills are essential for success in the workplace regardless of your major. *[Source: the Secretary's Commission on Achieving Necessary Skills (SCANS).]*

Foundation Skills
Basic Skills:

Reading
Writing
Basic arithmetic
Higher level mathematics
Listening
Speaking

Thinking Skills:

Creative thinking
Decision making
Problem solving
Mental visualization
Knowing how to learn
Reasoning

Personal Qualities:

Responsibility
Self-esteem
Sociability
Self-discipline
Integrity/honesty

WORKPLACE COMPETENCIES
Resources

- Time. Selects relevant goals, sets priorities, and follows a schedule.
- Money. Uses budgets, keeps records, and makes adjustments as required.
- Materials and facilities. Acquires, stores, and distributes supplies, parts, equipment, space, and/or final product
- Human resources. Assesses knowledge and skills, distributes work, evaluates performance, and provides constructive feedback

Interpersonal

- Participates as a member of a team. Works cooperatively with others and contributes to group efforts.
- Teaches others. Helps colleagues, clients, and others learn needed skills.
- Provides customer service. Works and communicates to deliver quality service to clients and customers and to satisfy their expectations.

- Exercises leadership. Communicates, encourages, persuades, and convinces others of worthy goals and strategies.
- Takes responsibility. Challenges procedures, policies, or authority where appropriate.
- Negotiates to arrive at a decision. Works toward agreement where there are diverging interests
- Embraces cultural diversity. Works well with men and women from a variety of ethnic, social, and educational backgrounds.

Information

- Acquires and evaluates information. Identifies the need for information, obtains it, and evaluates it.
- Organizes and maintains information. Sorts, processes, and maintains written and computerized records and documents.
- Uses computers to process information. Employs computers to acquire, organize, analyze, and communicate information.

Systems

- Understands systems. Knows how social, organizational, and technological systems work and operates effectively within them.
- Monitors and corrects performance. Distinguishes trends, predicts impacts of actions on systems operations, and takes action to correct performance.
- Improves systems. Develops new systems to improve products or services.

Technology

- Selects technology. Judges which procedures, tools, or machines, including computer, will produce the desired results.
- Applies technology to tasks. Understands proper procedures for using machines and computers.
- Maintains and troubleshoots technology. Prevents, identifies, and solves problems with machines, computers, and other technologies.

As the workforce continues to change, these information-related skills may well become more sought-after than the academic background acquired via a college major. If you strive to develop these skills, you'll be well prepared for the workforce.

What's more, the U.S. workforce is becoming increasingly diverse. Diversity includes many demographic variables, including race, religion, color, gender, age, national origin, disability, and sexual orientation. An appreciation for diversity is essential for maintaining a work environment that is open and allowing of individual difference. The fact that workplace diversity is increasing means new opportunity for many. It also means that a good education includes developing the ability to have productive working relationships with all kinds of people. Please refer to the chapter on Diversity for more information.

The U.S. Department of Labor's Bureau of Labor Statistics has identified these trends affecting the workplace:

- From 1998 to 2008, total employment was projected to increase from 140.5 million to 160.8 million, an increase of 14.4%.
- Due to the aging of the Baby Boomers, the average age of workers will rise. The median age for workers in 2000 was 39.
- More women will enter the workforce. Women now comprise 47% to 50% of American workers. Because they are still concentrated in traditionally "female" professions, they earn just 76 cents for every dollar earned by a man.
- One-third of new workers will be minorities. Hispanics and African Americans will continue to increase their representation in the workforce.
- There will be more immigrants than at any time since World War I.

Technology has revolutionized the workforce. Email, for instance, has made communication faster than ever and the Internet has become a conduit for the rapid delivery of goods and services. The paperless office is the wave of the future. Intranet usage has made it easier for workers to access, organize, and file data speedily and efficiently.

Today, as the U.S. evolves into an information society, increasingly fewer people work in agriculture and manufacturing. Many more enter service, technology, and information occupations. Such futurists as John Naisbitt, Patricia Aburdeen, and Walter Krechel note that we're moving toward a service economy based on high technology, rapid communication, health care, sales, and biotechnology for use in agriculture and medicine. Four of every five new jobs are in the service area, including health care, business education, wholesale and retail trade, finance, insurance, real estate, transportation, communication, public utilities, and government.

According to the U.S. Department of Labor, most job growth since 1970 has been in the service area. Those projected to increase in the coming decades:

- Health care professions will increase faster than any other service area. Two factors contributing to this growth: an aging population with a greater need for care, and advances in technology and medication resulting in higher-quality health services.
- Business functions such as data processing, advertising, and security will continue to be outsourced.
- Home functions such as cooking and cleaning will be contracted to service agencies. Trends suggest that Americans will increase their patronage of restaurants and related food industries.
- There will be an increasing demand for child care, nursing homes, and home health care services.
- The fastest-growing occupations between 1998 and 2008 have proven to be computer related: computer engineering, computer support, computer system analysis, database administration, and desktop publishing.

Employers increasingly employ nontraditional workers, including those holding multiple part-time jobs, contingent and part-time workers, independent contractors, and temporary employees. Unlike traditional workers, nontraditional workers do not have full-time, year-round jobs with health and retirement benefits. Nearly four out of five employers use nontraditional workers to cut costs, prevent layoffs, and access workers with special skills. There are advantages and disadvantages to this. Nontraditional workers have no benefits and risk unemployment, but they also tend to have flexible work schedules and can pursue other interests or gain new skills when not on the job.

Self Directed Search Results

Your letters:

What careers would you enjoy, based on the SDS assessment?

_____

_____

_____

_____

After learning your personality type and assessing your strengths and interests, the next step is to research your options and consider how each will reflect your personal values—or fail to do so. Many resources can assist you in exploring specific occupations. You can find the following references in TCC's Library and Career Center:

- *Occupational Outlook Handbook*
- *Career Information Center*
- *Encyclopedia of Career and Vocational Guidance*
- *Best Jobs of the 21st Century*

Research the following to better understand what each career entails:

- Type of education and degree required
- Average salary range in your region
- Average salary range nationwide
- Range of job opportunities in your field
- Employment trends—does your field have a future?
- Personality types suitable for the line of work
- General knowledge, skills, and abilities (KSA) needed to do the job well

Your values reflect what matters most to you, and your work ethic reflects the importance you attach to whatever you do for a living. If you identify your values now, you'll find it easier down the road to understand the nature of your work-related needs and long-term satisfaction. The intensity of your feelings reflects the strength of your values.

Values differ from facts and opinions; they're *your* standards for personal and professional behavior. Values are the things in life you want, just because you want them. They are the reference guiding your behavior, your choices, and your state of mind. All your values together comprise your *value system*. Values define who you are and who you want to be.

Therefore, having goals based on your value system will make your desire to achieve them stronger and you'll be more motivated to spend the time and effort needed to reach them.

LIFELONG EDUCATION

In the past, the traditional American's life pattern was to graduate, get a job, work for decades, and eventually retire. However, due to rapid changes in technology and society, workers now require additional training and education over the course of their careers. Continuing education takes a variety of forms: community college courses, on-the-job training, private lessons, and teaching oneself via the library, Internet, and other resources. Those who don't keep up with the new technology will find that their skills become obsolete. Those who do will find their skills in demand.

While most of the fastest-growing occupations require at least an associate's degree, three of four U.S. jobs do not require a bachelor's degree. Instead, they rely on short-term and on-the-job training. Prospective employees will need good skills in reading, communications, and math to take advantage of these training opportunities.

How might this trend affect your future?

_____

_____

MARKETING YOURSELF

Having planned your education and potential career, it's time to market yourself. Please refer to the chapter on Goal Setting and Choosing a Major for additional information. Here are some tools to acquire and use as you enter the workforce. Send a cover letter and résumé to potential employers as you search for a job. Remember: the key function of these documents is to get you an interview—nothing more, nothing less.

Your résumé summarizes your qualifications and work experience. Done right, it creates a favorable impression. Start compiling your information now (job dates, references) so that you'll be prepared when the time comes. A résumé is a work in progress. It's very important to save yours on a portable storage device, such as a disk or a thumb drive—with a backup—so that you can update it periodically.

To begin, here are a few helpful hints to use to as you develop your résumé:

- Visit the TCC Career Center for help with building your resume.
- Use a professional email address.
- Use premium white or off-white paper.
- Use only three font sizes (your name in 14-point, headings in 11-point, and content in 10-point).
- One sheet is preferred, but two sheets are acceptable if they are two full pages.
- To avoid having your email address underlined, remove the hyperlink.

- Do not staple your résumé or cover letter—use a paper clip.
- If mailing your résumé and cover letter, do not fold them. Mail them flat in a large manila envelope; when hand delivering, use a manila folder.
- Put a space under each heading.
- Remember to use the correct two-letter state abbreviations. Your best resource is your local post office if you are unsure of the correct abbreviations to use. Sometimes they are also listed in your local phone book.
- Do not include such personal data as age, race, religion, sexual orientation, marital status, etc.
- *Most importantly, make sure that you have someone proofread your résumé before you submit it.*

Your résumé can be formatted in many ways. The four major formats are chronological, functional, combination, and electronic résumés. A chronological résumé is the most traditional of all the formats. This type of résumé is organized by your employment history in reverse chronological order (most recent employment listed first), with job titles, names of employers, locations of employers, dates of employment, and accomplishments. You will also be able to list volunteer activities, education, community service, awards/honors, and other experiences in reverse chronological order as well. The chronological résumé is preferred by the widest variety of employers.

The advantages of a chronological format are that it is the simplest and quickest to develop and also provides the prospective employer with details of your employment history. The disadvantage to this format is that job seekers' gaps in employment and lack of work experience can easily be seen. For those job seekers who want to downplay their gaps in employment or lack of work experience, the functional résumé format may be the best choice.

Using the functional format, job seekers organize their résumés by skills and functions. In these résumés, company names, employment dates, and position titles are intentionally omitted. As previously mentioned, the most obvious advantage to using this format is that job seekers can present accomplishments from life experiences and minimizes job gaps that are more easily noticed in the chronological format. This format works well for new graduates entering the job market. A disadvantage of the functional format is that employers usually don't prefer it because it downplays details that they may use to narrow down the pool of candidates. Also, this version can be harder to write.

The combination résumé is a blend of both the chronological and functional formats. The combination format allows a job seeker to highlight outstanding skills and achievements and satisfies the potential employer's desire to see names and dates of previous employers. This format suits a variety of job seekers' needs. Job seekers who have large employment gaps or many short employment stints prefer this format because it downplays employment history. This type of résumé works well for people returning to the workforce, career changers, and job seekers with no degrees or limited experience.

There is one more type of résumé format that has come about due to the age of technology and the Internet. This format is called an electronic résumé. The electronic résumé is a vital tool for today's job seeker. But what exactly is an electronic résumé? Even among career experts, opinions vary about what is or is not an electronic résumé. It's a broadly used term that covers several types of résumés.

Job seekers are now placing résumés directly into searchable databases and more and more employers prefer to receive résumés by email. That means that it's an absolute must these days to have one of these types of electronic résumés.

- Text (ASCII) résumé, which removes all formatting and allows the résumé to appear the same in all email systems—and allows for easy placement into employer résumé databases.
- Rich Text (RTF) versions, sometimes used for online job boards (such as Monster, Careerbuilder, HotJobs) or for sending as an attachment that is reasonably compatible across platforms and word-processing programs.
- Portable Document Format (PDF), also highly compatible and consistent in appearance across platforms, though difficult to place directly into databases.
- Web-based résumé in hypertext markup language (HTML) to make your résumé available 24/7 on the Web. Easily expandable into a Web portfolio.
- Scannable résumé, which is similar to a text résumé although used increasingly less often these days since emailed résumés can go directly into databases and don't require the extra step of optical scanning.

As you might imagine, any number of versions of your résumé are possible, including chronological, functional, combination, or electronic formats. You could, for example, have both chronological and functional versions of your résumé in print, RTF, PDF, HTML, and scannable file formats. In fact, preparing more than one version of your résumé is a smart idea. You never know when you may be asked to email your résumé on short notice when you thought you would only need a printed one on hand.

To start your résumé, fill out the following worksheet:

GETTING STARTED ON YOUR RÉSUMÉ
Personal

Full Name: Phone: (   )   -
Address: City: State: Zip:
Email address:

Education

School Name: *Tallahassee Community College*

City, State: *Tallahassee, FL*

Degree: *Associate of Arts, Associate of Science,* or *Applied Associate of Science* (circle one)

Major: GPA (optional):

Year Graduated (or expected to graduate):

High School Name or GED:

City, State:

Degree: *Diploma*

GPA (optional):   Year Graduated:

Related activities, volunteer experiences and accomplishments

_____

_____

Work Experience (Start with your current or most recent job)

Name of Company or Organization:

City, State:

Date Started: Date Ended (or present):

Job Title:

Job Description: (What do/did you do? Use key words. Be clear and concise. Emphasize results and accomplishments! Use numbers and percentages wherever possible.)

_____

_____

Next most recent job:

Name of Company or Organization:

City, State:

Date Started: Date Ended (or present):

Job Title:

Job Description:

_____

_____

Next most recent job:

Name of Company or Organization:

City, State:

Date Started: Date Ended (or present):

Job Title:

Job Description:

_____

_____

Next most recent job:

Name of Company or Organization:

City, State:

Date Started: Date Ended (or present):

Job Title:

Job Description:

_____

_____

Training and Workshops

_____

_____

Other Job Skills (typing, shorthand, computer skills, the ability to operate machines, languages spoken, etc.):

_____

_____

Awards, Honors and Achievements:

_____

_____

Professional organizations, civic groups and clubs:

_____

_____

Special Skills/Technical Skills, etc.

_____

_____

WRITING A COVER LETTER

When you submit your résumé, send your cover letter as well. The letter will introduce you to a prospective employer and highlight the skills you want that person to consider. The cover letter also shows your ability to communicate in writing.

Before starting your cover letter, however, do your research. Find out everything you can about the organization you're thinking of working for. Most important: the job description or announcement, which will help you select those skills and qualifications to mention in your letter. A cover letter should be no more than one page. Many formats are acceptable.

Here are a few tips for writing a cover letter:

1. A cover letter should be no more than one page.

2. Use standard business format.

3. Make sure you sign your letter.

4. If mailing your résumé and cover letter, do not fold them. Mail your documents flat in a large manila envelope. When hand delivering, use a manila folder.

5. Try to find out to whom the letter should be addressed; avoid using the phrase "To Whom It May Concern."

6. Make sure you proofread; grammatical or spelling errors can lose you the job!

Now, let's hope—after sending a letter requesting an interview—that you get that all-important call. If you do, congratulations! Your résumé and cover letter served their purpose—to get you in the door. Now, the interview is your chance to make a lasting impression, market yourself, evaluate the position, and demonstrate your personal qualities and communication skills.

Here is a general outline for any type of cover letter:

Date you are writing the letter

Your Present Address
City, State, Zip Code

Your addressee's name
Professional title
Organization name
Mailing address
City, state and zip

Dear Mr. (or Ms.) last name:

First Paragraph: State your reason for writing and specify clearly the position or field for which you are applying. Tell how you heard about the opening or organization.

Second Paragraph: State why you are interested in the position, the organization, its products or services. This lets the employer know that you've researched the company on your own, that you're thorough, and a self-starter.

Third Paragraph: Emphasize how your academic background, college activities and work experience qualifies you as a candidate. You should not summarize your résumé.

Final Paragraph: Refer the employer to your enclosed documents. Indicate your desire for a personal interview and your flexibility as to time and place. Then also express appreciation to the reader for his (or her) time and consideration.

Sincerely,

Your handwritten signature

Your name (typed)

Enclosure—This refers to the documents you will send with this cover letter.

HERE'S HOW TO PREPARE FOR A JOB INTERVIEW

Any competent employer looks for the best people to hire. Your job is to show the interviewer that you are that person. You can demonstrate what you have to offer the organization by discussing your education and experience. Remember, the interview is your chance to shine, and you only get one—make it count!

Part of preparing for an interview is to anticipate what you may be asked. You'll probably be questioned about your education, aspirations, personality, and goals. The better prepared you are, the more easily your responses will come in the interview. The best way to prepare is by practicing. Here are some questions typically asked in interviews and some suggestions for answering them:

1. Tell us about yourself.

Think about the job requirements. Bear in mind that interviewers are looking for someone who will do a good job for the company. Talk about your education and experience as they relate to the job. Include interesting facts about your life and hobbies, but keep your answers brief. This question is generally an ice-breaker to help the interviewer get a general picture of you.

2. Why do you want this job? Why should I hire you?

Think about the research you did on this company and how you could contribute as an employee. A good answer might be, "I have always been good at technical skills and engineering. I am interested in putting these skills into practice in your company." An inappropriate answer would be, "I want to make lots of money and need health insurance."

3. Why are you leaving your present job?

Rather than saying that your boss is horrible and the working conditions intolerable, (even if true), think of positive reasons for leaving, such as:

- I'm looking for a job that provides challenge and opportunity for growth.
- I've received my degree and am looking for a job where I can put my education to use.
- I had a part-time job to help me through school, but now I've graduated and am looking for a professional career.
- I moved (or the company downsized or went out of business).

Be careful about discussing problems on a previous job. The interviewers might assume that you were to blame or that you couldn't get along with your former colleagues.

4. What are your strengths and weaknesses?

Think about your strengths in relation to the job requirements and be prepared to talk about them during the interview. When asked about your weaknesses smile and turn them into strengths. For example, if you're an introvert, you might say that while you're quiet and like to concentrate on your tasks, you nonetheless make an effort to communicate with others. If you're an extrovert, say that you enjoy talking and working with others, but are good at time management and getting the job done. If you're a perfectionist, explain that while you like to do an excellent job, you also grasp the importance of deadlines and do the best you can in the time available.

5. Tell us about a difficult situation or problem that you solved on the job.

Think about problems you solved on the job and describe how you did it. Focus on what you accomplished. If the problem dealt with other people, do not focus on blaming or complaining. Instead, concentrate on your desire to work things out and work well with everyone.

6. Tell us about one of your achievements on the job.

Give examples of projects you have done that have turned out well and that gave you a sense of pride and achievement.

7. What do you like best about your work? What do you like least?

Think about these questions in advance and use the questions to highlight your skills. For the question about what you like the least, be honest but express your willingness to do the job that is required.

QUESTIONS TO ASK DURING AN INTERVIEW

Remember, an interview is a two-way exchange. In the first part, you're the interviewee. Then you become the interviewer! After asking your questions, the interviewer usually invites you to ask some. By responding with well-informed, well-thought-out questions (such as the following), you'll not only learn what you need to know about the potential job and employer, you'll also make a good impression.

Here are some questions you can ask the interviewer:

- What is a typical workday like?
- Does the company plan to expand in the next 3 years?
- What are the significant trends in the industry?
- What are the projects for which I would first be responsible?
- When will you be making a decision?

Name three additional questions to ask a prospective employer:

1. _____

2. _____

3. _____

THE INTERVIEW

The importance of learning about the job and organization *before* the interview can't be overemphasized. It will help you in two ways: you'll know if the job is really for you, and you'll have information to make the interview a success. Having researched the company before the interview, you'll make a good impression and demonstrate your interest.

These suggestions will help make your interview a successful one:

1. Research the company before your interview.
2. Know where the interview will take place and arrive on time, if not early.
3. Use a firm handshake when you meet the interviewer(s).
4. Make direct eye contact with your interviewer(s).
5. Be aware of your nonverbal communications.
6. Don't slouch in your chair; sit appropriately.
7. Wait for the end of each question to begin your answer. Don't cut off the person asking the question.
8. Don't bring up salary.

FIRST IMPRESSIONS

LaShondra, a pre-med student, and Mary, who wants to be a teacher, are looking for part-time jobs while in college. Both have applied to a local office as a receptionist and both have interviews this afternoon. Mary is coming straight from a class at TCC while LaShondra arranged her interview for a day when she didn't have classes. The hiring manager has looked at both resumes and knows his decision is going to come down to which makes the best impression because they are both well qualified for the job. LaShondra's interview is first and she arrives 15 minutes early because she doesn't want to take a chance on being late. She has been very careful with how she dressed today making sure that her skirt is not too short and that her blouse, while stylish, is not too low cut. Her make-up is lightly done, her hair is pulled back, and her nails are clean and well manicured. Mary, on the other hand, arrives 5 minutes after her interview should have begun because her class ran long. She didn't have a chance to go home and change clothes but she isn't worried. She has on her best pair of jeans, nice and snug, just like she likes them. Her shirt, though tight, is not low cut and her flip flops match her outfit. She doesn't wear make-up to school so she dabs on a little as she walks into the office. Her hair really needs to be combed and her manicure needs work, but she knows that she can do the job, so no worries. The hiring manager interviews both young ladies who do equally well with his questions. Who do you think got the job?

Dressing the part

What do you consider appropriate dress for an interview?

_____

_____

_____

MEN'S ATTIRE
Polo shirt, Khakis, Dark socks, and leather shoes
Dress shirt, Tie, Dress Pants, Dark socks, and leather shoes
Minimal jewelry
Professional hairstyle or well kept hair
Nicely trimmed nails and light cologne

WOMEN'S ATTIRE
Nice dress that is knee length
Dark Suit and coordinating blouse
If suit is a skirt it should be at the knee
Conservative shoes like pumps with pantyhose
Light make-up and cologne
Clean nails and nicely styled hair

How do you look?

Making a good first impression can be the difference between getting a job and not getting a job. In today's job market you need to take advantage of every opportunity you can to make a lasting impression and how you dress does that. Although you may think the job is only part-time or only entry level so what does it matter, showing up for an interview looking good does play a part in how you are perceived. While the job you're applying for may not require a tie, wearing one to the interview shows respect to the hiring person. And, even though you may never wear pumps or dress shoes, an interviewer is going to think much more of those than your favorite flip flops or flats. Although you may regard your cell phone, iPod, and multiple earrings or piercings as great fashion accessories, the person doing the hiring doesn't. Neither are they going to appreciate the rad tattoo on your arm, leg, or wherever. Make sure those are covered, too, and leave those other items at home. Above are some guidelines for you to use for dressing when interviewing.

Types of Interviews

In today's electronic society the term interview has taken on new meaning. While some jobs still require a face-to-face interview with the hiring manager, you may also experience some other types of interviews. Among those are:

Screening interviews—This type of interview can be done either in person or on the phone. The purpose of this interview is to match the capabilities of potential employees with the needs of the company. When conducted over the phone these are often done unexpectedly, so keep your information handy. When asked to come in for a screening interview, treat it just like an interview with the hiring manager.

Selection interviews—This is the interview where you meet with the decision maker or a committee or have several interviews one after another so that the people you are working for get a chance to meet you, talk with you, and determine not only your qualifications but also how well you fit in with the other members of the team. Be sure to be yourself and to establish rapport with the hiring person so that you can establish your ability to do the job.

Follow-up

After your interview, send a thank-you note. That gives you an advantage over other candidates for the job, since the note reminds the employer of you and your application. When writing the note, thank the interviewer for his or her time and mention your interest in the position and value to the company. Keep the note brief!

A thank you letter can be typed, handwritten, or emailed. A handwritten note is acceptable, but if your penmanship is lacking, type a letter. And be sure you sign it. Email thank you notes are appropriate when your means of contact with the employer has been via email or if your contact has expressed a preference for email. You can also send a quick email thank you to be followed up by a handwritten note.

Here is a general outline that can be used for typing a thank you letter.

Date you are writing the letter
Your Present Address
City, State, Zip Code

Your addressee's name
Professional title
Organization name
Mailing address
City, State, Zip Code

Dear Mr. (or Ms.) last name:

First Paragraph: Thank the interviewer for taking the time to meet with you.

Second Paragraph: Mention your interest in the job and how enthusiastic you are about it. In this paragraph, you can mention anything you might want the employer to know that you did not mention during your interview.

Third Paragraph: You should include the reasons why you are an excellent candidate for the job. List specific skills that relate to the job you interviewed for. The more detailed you are, the more the interviewer will know about your qualifications.

Final Paragraph: Indicate your appreciation for being considered for the position and let the interviewer know you look forward to hearing from him (or her) soon.

Sincerely,

Your handwritten signature

Your name (typed)

Of course, following all the steps outlined in this chapter doesn't guarantee that you'll get your dream job on the first try. Other applicants may have more experience than you, or fill a special niche the employer was seeking. Sometimes, of course, the employer just chooses someone else. Don't be discouraged. The average job seeker applies to 23 different companies before they are hired.

But when the person hired is you, it feels great! *You* delivered a well-designed cover letter, impressive résumé, dynamic interview, and appealing thank-you note. You're now equipped to interact in today's competitive job market!

SUMMARY

After graduation, you'll find yourself in the "world of work." Your academic success will be the basis for your career success. Employers look for many skills, so by exploring them as a student, you'll be prepared. A strong résumé and cover letter are essential for creating a positive impression on a potential employer. Follow them up with a solid interview to reinforce that strong impression in person. Don't be discouraged if you don't get every job you apply for; even with a great résumé, cover letter, and interview, you may still be turned down. After all, there are sometimes hundreds of applicants for one position. However, you'll be honing your skills with practice. And remember: a good résumé and cover letter will guarantee a second glance from an employer and sometimes that's the edge you need to get the position you want!

CHRONOLOGICAL RESUMÉ EXAMPLE

Nicole S. Kalogeras
1234 Main Street
Tallahassee, FL 32304
Home: (850) 555-5555
Cell: (850) 555-5555
email@tcc.fl.edu

Education
Associate of Arts 2011
Tallahassee Community College, Tallahassee, Florida

Experience
Wonderful Memories Resort, Tallahassee, FL
PBX Operator and Front Desk, April 2007–present
- Ensure guest satisfaction through telephone service with promptness and in a courteous manner
- Promote the resort, the facilities and activities on the property
- Provide information regarding local attractions and events
- Check guests in and out of the resort
- Arrange transportation for guests when necessary
- Work in conjunction with the bell staff to assist guests to their rooms
- Handle cash and credit card transactions
- Run various reports—handwritten and computer

A-OK-ValueMART, Tallahassee, FL
Sales Clerk, September 2006–March 2007
- Assisted in re-merchandising the store
- Priced inventory
- Utilized loss prevention skills
- Communicated with vendors
- Gained experience in selling and customer service
- Used a register in the store including cash, check and credit card transactions
- Maintained organizational tasks in the store.

Tallahassee School, Tallahassee, FL
Summer Recreation Counselor, June 2006–August 2006
- Assisted in planning, coordinating and directing recreation and athletic programs
- Ensured proper safety and risk management procedures
- Oversaw 25 children between the ages of 6 to 13 years old
- Facilitated a room when we were on campus which included arts and crafts, games and movies
- Developed themes for the days: i.e., music, cars, team building, communication and future goals
- Directed and supervised fieldtrip program
- Evaluated recreation program and discussed it with the program director

McDermott Brothers Landscaping—Private Estate Work, Tallahassee, FL
Gardener, 2004–2005 summer months
- Worked on estates doing landscaping work and maintenance

Computer Skills
Windows Me   MS Word   MS Excel   MS PowerPoint   Publisher

FUNCTIONAL RESUMÉ EXAMPLE

LILLIAN MIHALIK

1234 Main Street • Tallahassee, Florida 32304 • (850) 222-2222 • email@hotmail.com

PROFESSIONAL EXPERIENCE

Office Management
- Established procedures to improve office efficiency
- Maintained payroll and tax records
- Communicated with customer personally and by correspondence

Accounting
- Set up and maintained a computer system that resulted in a 15% savings
- Monitored and handled budget requisitions and budget amendments for accounts

Event Management
- Supervised part-time staff during special events for the cities of Jacksonville and Tallahassee
- Assisted with coordination of banquet and special events that raised $5000.00 for different charities

Marketing
- Served as a phone-a-thon caller on several occasions, soliciting donations from FSU and FAMU alumni
- Formatted/designed and wrote advertisements for a weekly newspaper which reached 20,000 local households
- Development of web pages for local business advertisers

Personnel Management
- Recruited, hired, and trained staff of 20
- Worked effectively with an interdisciplinary team

COMPUTER SKILLS

Windows, MS Word, MS Excel, MS PowerPoint, Publisher, Internet skills

RELEVANT COURSES

Financial Accounting	Introduction to Human Relations
Introduction to Management	Marketing the Individual
Managerial Accounting	Strategic Planning
Webpage Development	Principle of Advertising

EDUCATION

Associate of Science, Business Management, April 2011
Tallahassee Community College
Tallahassee, FL

COMBINATION RESUMÉ EXAMPLE

Marcus Simpson
1234 Main Street
Tallahassee, FL 32304
Home: (850) 555-5555
Cell: (954) 555-5555
email@tcc.fl.edu

Summary of Skills

Verbal communication	Written communication	Customer service
Time management	Sales	Marketing
Organizational	Leadership	Research
Event management	Planning	Networking
Computer Skills		

Education

Associate of Arts, anticipated April 2010
Tallahassee Community College, Tallahassee, Florida

High School Diploma, May 2006
Lauderdale Shores High School, Fort Lauderdale, FL

Experience

A-OK-ValueMART, Tallahassee, FL
Sales Associate and Cashier, September 2006–present

Happy Hamburger Restaurant, Tallahassee, FL
Shift Supervisor, August 2005–March 2006

Shadewell Country Club, Tallahassee, FL
Caddie, May 2005–August 2005

Fun in the Sun Summer Day Camp, Fort Lauderdale, FL
Camp Counselor, June 2004–August 2004

Volunteer Experience and College Activities

Habitat for Humanity
American Heart Walk
Capital Area Chapter of the American Red Cross
Tallahassee Community College, Black Male Achievers, member
Tallahassee Community College, Intramural Sport Participant—Basketball and Soccer
Outdoor Recreation Community Volunteer Club, member
Student Government Association, member

Certifications

CPR and First Aid

Honors and Achievements

TCC Alumni Association Book Scholarship Recipient
Dean's List Fall 2009 and Spring 2010

Chapter 14

The Dimensions of Wellness

LEARNING OBJECTIVES

By the end of this chapter you should be able to:

Describe how the physical, emotional and social parts of the person work together

Explain the effects of drugs and alcohol on the self

Foster healthy relationships

Solve problems effectively

THE PHYSICAL

How are you? You probably answered "Fine"—without really thinking. Chances are, though, that you haven't considered what constitutes your true well-being. How do you **really** feel . . . about yourself, your life, your health? Do you eat well? Do you exercise often? Do you smoke or drink? Do you have close friends with whom you share your experiences? Are you under stress to get good grades, perform well at work, or be a good parent? Do you get regular medical checkups and practice self-care? Do you know about safety and environmental issues affecting your health? This chapter will help you develop strategies to live life to the fullest, both physically and emotionally.

Nutrition

According to the Centers for Disease Control and Prevention, 64.5% of U.S. adults aged 20 and older are overweight; 30.5% are obese. Obesity increases the risk of illness from at least 30 serious medical conditions, of impaired mobility, and of discrimination in workplace, academic, and social settings.

Why does this matter to you, especially if you're young and burn up everything you eat? For many American adults, as much as 40% of the calories they consume come from fat. Obesity is usually the result of a combination: poor diet and inactivity. And since most students have busy schedules, they tend to neglect their diets (and workouts). Most are on tight budgets, so they fill up on starch, which costs less than fruit, vegetables, lean meat, or fish.

By taking time to improve your diet, however, you can boost your daily performance and enhance your sense of well-being.

The basic ingredients of a healthy diet are summarized in the food pyramid (see Figure 14-1); a guide to making daily food choices that was developed by the U.S. Departments of Agriculture and Health and Human Services.

- Reduce the fat in your diet to less than 30% of your total calories, with less than 10% coming from saturated or animal fats. By cutting back on whole-milk dairy products, fatty meats, mayonnaise, and butter, you can reduce your fat intake significantly! Many students snack while doing homework, but you can replace those potato chips with fruit or unbuttered popcorn. The idea is to cut back on fats, but not eliminate them; some is good for you.

- Consume a variety of foods from the five food groups: fruit; vegetables; dairy; whole grain cereals, bread, and pasta; and lean meats such as poultry and fish. If red meat is the source of protein you prefer, select only lean cuts.

- Eat a balance of foods, but emphasize vegetables, fruit, and grain products.

- Be moderate in your consumption of table sugar (and other sugary items such as honey) as well as salt. Many students fall prey to consuming soft drinks and candy bars because of their easy availability. Try substituting water and a small bag of low-salt or no-salt pretzels.

- Avoid alcohol. When you do consume it, moderation is the key: no more than two drinks in a 24-hour period.

- Drink lots of water! Eight glasses a day is recommended. Water is especially important before, during, and after exercise.

- Eat breakfast. It really is the most important meal, providing an energy boost to get you on track for a productive day. And having protein for breakfast gives you stamina to maintain your performance. Remember: sugar and caffeine for breakfast will give you short-term energy, but you're likely to be tired and hungry well before lunch. Nor is skipping meals and catching up later a good approach to nutrition.

Anatomy of MyPyramid

One size doesn't fit all
USDA's new MyPyramid symbolizes a personalized approach to healthy eating and physical activity. The symbol has been designed to be simple. It has been developed to remind consumers to make healthy food choices and to be active every day. The different parts of the symbol are described below.

Activity
Activity is represented by the steps and the person climbing them, as a reminder of the importance of daily physical activity.

Moderation
Moderation is represented by the narrowing of each food group from bottom to top. The wider base stands for foods with little or no solid fats or added sugars. These should be selected more often. The narrower top area stands for foods containing more added sugars and solid fats. The more active you are, the more of these foods can fit into your diet.

Personalization
Personalization is shown by the person on the steps, the slogan, and the URL. Find the kinds and amounts of food to eat each day at MyPyramid.gov.

Proportionality
Proportionality is shown by the different widths of the food group bands. The widths suggest how much food a person should choose from each group. The widths are just a general guide, not exact proportions. Check the Web site for how much is right for you.

Variety
Variety is symbolized by the 6 color bands representing the 5 food groups of the Pyramid and oils. This illustrates that foods from all groups are needed each day for good health.

Gradual Improvement
Gradual improvement is encouraged by the slogan. It suggests that individuals can benefit from taking small steps to improve their diet and lifestyle each day.

MyPyramid.gov
STEPS TO A HEALTHIER YOU

USDA U.S. Department of Agriculture
Center for Nutrition Policy
and Promotion
April 2005 CNPP-16

USDA is an equal opportunity provider and employer.

GRAINS VEGETABLES FRUITS OILS MILK MEAT& BEANS

Figure 14-1 Anatomy of MyPyramid

Understanding the information on food product labels will help you practice good nutrition. The parts of a typical label are shown in Figure 14-2 and are described in detail in Table 14-1, along with recommendations on how to use the information.

Eating Disorders

Eating disorders are real, treatable medical illnesses with complex underlying psychological and biological causes. They frequently coexist with other psychiatric disorders such as depression, substance abuse, or anxiety disorders. People with eating disorders also can suffer from numerous other physical health complications, such as heart conditions or kidney failure, which can lead to death.

WHAT THE LABEL MEANS

Serving size. Is your serving the same size as the one on the label? If you eat double the serving listed, then calculate your intake by doubling the nutrient and calorie values as well. If you eat half the serving size shown, divide the nutrient and calorie values by two.

Calories. A 5'4", 135-pound, active woman needs about 2,200 calories each day. A 5'10", 174-pound, active man needs about 2,900. Here's how a serving of food adds to your daily total:

> **Total carbohydrate.** When you cut down on fat, you can eat more carbohydrates. Carbohydrates are found in bread, potatoes, fruits and vegetables. Choose these often! They give you nutrients and energy.

> **Dietary fiber.** In the past people called it "roughage." Today, research shows the value of both soluble and insoluble dietary fiber: fruit, vegetables, whole-grain foods, beans and peas. Fiber appears to lower the risks of cancer and heart disease.

> **Protein.** Most Americans get more protein than they need. Where there is animal protein, there is also cholesterol and fat! So eat small servings of lean meat, fish and poultry, and use skim or low-fat milk, yogurt and cheese. You can also substitute such vegetable proteins as beans, grains and cereals.

> **Vitamins and minerals.** Your goal here is 100 percent of each, every day. Don't count on one food to do it all. Instead, eat meals that supply the vitamins and minerals you need. Remember, if you take a vitamin pill, your body will retain more of its value when you've also eaten.

> **Total fat.** Aim low for this category. Most people need to cut back on fat; too much has been linked to heart disease and cancer. For a healthy heart, choose foods with a big difference between the total number of calories and the number of calories from fat. Try to limit your calories from fat.

> **Saturated fat.** Saturated fat is part of the total fat in food. It is listed separately because it is the key player in raising blood cholesterol and your risk of heart disease. Aim to eat less.

> **Cholesterol.** Too much cholesterol—second cousin to fat—can lead to heart disease. Challenge yourself to eat less than 300 milligrams each day.

> **Sodium.** You call it "salt," the label calls it "sodium." Either way, it adds up to high blood pressure for many. So keep your sodium intake low—2,400 to 3,000 milligrams or less each day for healthy adults.

Daily value. Drowning in numbers? Let the Daily Value be your guide. Daily Values are listed for people who eat 2,000 to 2,500 calories each day. If you eat more, your personal daily value may be higher than that listed on the label; if you eat less, it may be lower. For fat, saturated fat, cholesterol and sodium, choose foods with a low percent Daily Value. For total carbohydrates, dietary fiber, vitamins and minerals, your goal is to reach 100 percent in each category.

Source: Food and Drug Administration. (N. D.). How to Read the New Food Label (FDA 93-2260). Dallas, TX: National Center.

If you think you may be experiencing an eating disorder or know someone who is, there are many sources for help. The best place to begin is with the Mental Health Counseling department we discussed in the chapter on campus resources.

Exercise

Essential to establishing a healthy lifestyle is exercise. Keep in mind that a fitness program that suits one person may not fit another—but do something! Your optimal level of exercise varies by age and current health status, but it's always advisable to engage a professional to help develop a program that meets your specific needs. Balance is important, so find yours somewhere between obsessive/compulsive workouts and no exercise at all.

With that word of caution, here are some fitness tips known to be beneficial.

- Do some type of aerobic exercise, such as walking, jogging, or swimming, for three 30-minute periods each week. If you find it more convenient to walk or jog near your home, don't do it alone, and let others know your routine; for instance, tell a roommate you are leaving to run. Human predators are sometimes attracted to campuses. To be safe, expect the worse.

    Also, be reasonable in your expectations. Recognize that while basketball may provide more exercise than golf or bowling, these latter types of exercise are still good for you.

- Consider riding a bicycle to, from, and around campus. (That will help your budget, too.)

- Walk instead of riding campus transportation, such as buses. Walking up and down the hills on a hilly campus (think Florida A&M) is great exercise!

- Instead of riding the elevator, take the stairs.

- Find ways to incorporate exercise into your daily routine. Instead of having a pizza delivered, take your class notes and quiz yourself as you walk to the neighborhood pizza parlor.

- Reduce or eliminate your consumption of substances, such as cigarettes and alcohol, that interfere with your ability to exercise.

- Get enough sleep. Being tired can dampen your motivation to exercise.

- Get regular medical checkups and screenings (e.g., mammograms). Your fitness regime should include seeing a physician. Find out about your current health, what maintenance measures you should take, and what should be done to correct any health problems.

Nutrition Facts

Serving Size ½ cup (114g)
Serving Per Container 4

Amount Per Serving

Calories 90   Calories from Fat 30

	% Daily Value*
Total Fat 3g	5%
Saturated Fat 0g	0%
Cholesterol 0mg	0%
Sodium 300mg	13%
Total Carbohydrate 13g	4%
Dietary Fiber 3g	12%
Sugars 3g	
Protein 3g	

Vitamin A	80%	•	Vitamin C	60%
Calcium	4%	•	Iron	4%

* Percent Daily Values are based on a 2,000 calorie diet. Your daily values may be higher or lower depending on your calorie needs:

	Calories	2,000	2,500
Total Fat	Less than	65g	80g
Sat Fat	Less than	20g	25g
Cholesterol	Less than	300mg	300mg
Sodium	Less than	2,400mg	2,400mg
Total Carbohydrate		300g	375g
Fiber		25g	30g

Calories per gram:
Fat 9   •   Carbohydrate 4   •   Protein 4

More nutrients may be listed on some labels.

Figure 14-2 A Typical Food Label

DAILY FOOD DIARY

Date: _____   Day of Week: _____

As most nutritionists will tell you, keeping track of the calories you consume is one of the most effective ways to lose and/or maintain healthy weight. Try it for one day. Use this chart to record everything you eat in one day. No cheating! Record every morsel. From the handful of nuts, to the candy bar on the way to school, the drinks at the club, and everything in between—write it down. This is the only way to truly know where you are in your weight program. Use a standard calorie counter or the label on your food to find calories per serving, and, if you eat more than one, don't forget to include that in your number.

	TIME OF DAY	WHAT I ATE	CALORIES
Breakfast			
Snack			
Lunch			
Snack			
Dinner			
Beverages			
Total Calories			

THE SOCIAL

Avoiding Addictions

Abusing alcohol or illegal drugs can limit your success in college, on the job, and in life. Addictions can also cause illness and shorten your life expectancy. Having good information will help you make the best choices.

Alcohol

Each year, many college students die because of excess drinking. Some die in alcohol-related auto accidents or acts of impaired judgment, such as leaping from a motel balcony during spring break. Others die from alcohol poisoning. Some even cause the deaths of others!

Excess drinking is also a factor in poor college performance and high dropout rates. Studies show that heavy drinking causes brain damage and interferes with memory.

Binge Drinking

Binge drinking is consuming too much alcohol at one time, and binge drinkers are at risk for many alcohol-related problems. In men, binge drinking is defined by researchers as five or more drinks in a row; in women, four or more. Since it takes about 1 hour to metabolize one drink, it takes 5 hours to metabolize five drinks. Researchers estimate that more than two of five college students (44%) are binge drinkers. Binge drinkers are 21 times more likely to:

- Be hurt or injured
- Drive a car after drinking
- Get in trouble with campus or local police
- Engage in unprotected sex
- Engage in unplanned sexual activity
- Damage property
- Fall behind in classes
- Miss class

It's critical to note the strong connection between binge drinking and driving. Among frequent binge drinkers, 62% of men and 49% of women say they have driven a car after drinking alcohol. About half the students in this study reported having been a passenger in a car in which the driver was drunk or high on drugs. And heavy drinking causes students to miss class and fall behind in their schoolwork.

Warning Signs of Alcoholism

Alcoholics Anonymous has published 12 questions to determine whether alcohol is a problem in your life. Answer these questions honestly:

1. Have you ever decided to stop drinking for a week or so but could only stop for a couple of days?

2. Do you wish people would mind their own business about your drinking and stop telling you what to do?

3. Have you ever switched from one kind of drink to another in the hope that this would keep you from getting drunk?

4. During the past year, have you ever had to have a drink upon awakening? Do you need a drink to get started or stop shaking?

5. Do you envy people who can drink without getting into trouble?

6. Have you had problems connected with drinking in the past year?

7. Has your drinking caused problems at home?

8. Do you ever try to get extra drinks at a party?

9. Do you tell yourself you can stop drinking any time you want, although you keep getting drunk when you don't plan to?

10. Have you missed work or school because of drinking?

11. Do you ever have blackouts from drinking and can't remember what happened?

12. Have you ever felt that your life would be better if you didn't drink?

If you answered yes to four of the above questions, it is likely that you have a problem with alcohol. If you do have a problem there are a number of resources on campus that can help you. Refer back to the chapter on campus resources for assistance.

Smoking

Cigarette smoking has been identified as the most important source of preventable morbidity (disease and illness) and premature mortality (death) worldwide. Smoking-related diseases claim an estimated 438,000 American lives each year, including those affected indirectly, such as babies born prematurely due to prenatal maternal smoking and victims of "secondhand" exposure to tobacco's carcinogens. Smoking cost the United States over $193 billion in 2004, including $97 billion in lost productivity and $96 billion in direct health care expenditures, or an average of $4,260 per adult smoker.

- If you smoke, stop or cut down with the aim of stopping. Approximately 45.1 million U.S. adults smoke cigarettes. Sixteen percent of youth smoke, compared to 12% of adults. According to the Centers for Disease Control and Prevention, roughly 438,000 Americans die prematurely each year from smoking or exposure to secondhand smoke, while another 8.6 million contract a serious illness caused by smoking. And for each person who dies from smoking, 20 more suffer from at least one serious tobacco-related illness.

Smoking also creates a huge economic burden, both for individuals and for the entire world. In the U.S. alone, medical expenditures for tobacco-related illness totaled more than $75 billion per year, while another $92 billion annually is the result of lost productivity.

Other Drugs

Alcohol is the most abused drug on college campuses, but prescription and street drugs are close behind. When students abuse drugs, their schoolwork, jobs, and relationships take a back seat to their all-consuming focus on procuring still more drugs. One of the worst effects of addictive behavior is the loss of ambition. Ambition inspires you to enjoy life and pursue happiness, but can be destroyed through drug use, which damages such vital functions as concentration and memory. These tools are essential to learning so, without them, your educational outlook is severely impaired.

Why Illegal Drugs Are Bad

1. They are illegal.
2. They are dangerous and can have negative health consequences.
3. There is no Quality Control used in their creation.
4. There is no warning sheet about other drug interactions.
5. No one monitors the non-negligible worry about allergic reactions.

People take drugs to feel better in the short-term. The problem is that, in the long-term, drugs can become life-destroying. Anyone contemplating taking drugs should ask these questions:

1. Will I experience more pleasure than pain, or more pain than pleasure?
2. Will the pleasure be temporary? How will I feel tomorrow?
3. Will the drug do more harm than good?

Answering these questions honestly can help you to make the right choices in determining the direction of your life.

Sex

Sex is not just physical; it has a whole array of personal, interpersonal, and familial meanings that have little to do with its actual physicality. Regardless of your views of sexuality—whether you believe in free love, waiting till marriage, or something in between—your knowledge of sexual health is important. And regardless of when you become sexually active, one concern with profound health and psychological consequences is that of sexually transmitted disease (STDs). College health centers provide information and services related to this and other aspects of sexual health.

STDs are common among young people

- About 333 million new cases of curable sexually transmitted diseases (STDs) occur each year among young adults around the world.
- One in five people in the United States has an STD.
- One in four new STD infections occurs in teenagers.
- One in four people will have an STD at some point during his or her life.
- One in 10 teenagers knows someone who is HIV-positive.
- Fifty-six percent of teenagers 12 to 17 years of age think STDs are a big problem for people their age.

Some STDs can be cured, but not all of them

There are two categories of STDs. Bacterial STDs are caused by bacteria while viral STDs are caused by viruses. As a result of being caused by different microorganisms, bacterial and viral STDs vary in their treatment:

- Bacterial STDs, such as gonorrhea, syphilis, and chlamydia, are cured with antibiotics.
- Viral STDs such as HIV, HPV (which causes genital warts), herpes, and hepatitis B— the four Hs—have no cure, but their symptoms can be reduced with treatment.

Some STDs have symptoms, but not all, and not all of the time

It is important to remember that some STDs cause no symptoms, and when symptoms do occur, they are often not recognized.

Most people with STDs have no symptoms—none! So you can be infected and infect someone else without knowing it. However, there are some common signs to watch for.

- The symptoms listed below are tricky. They can show up anywhere from 2 days to a couple of months after initial exposure to the disease. Sometimes, symptoms can show up as long as several years after the initial STD infection. Specific symptoms might include:

    Bumps or blisters near the mouth or genitals;

    Burning or pain during urination or a bowel movement; and

    Flu-like symptoms, including fever, chills, and aches, as well as swelling in the groin area.

If you notice any of these symptoms or think you may have been exposed to an STD, seek medical care as soon as possible.

STDs are preventable

- People can get STDs when they engage in vaginal, anal, or oral sex. The only sure way to prevent getting an STD is to not have sex. If you have sex with someone who has an STD, you can get it, too.
- Condoms can dramatically reduce your risk of contracting STDs when used consistently and correctly, but they don't provide 100 percent protection. Still, if you are going to have sex, make sure to protect yourself and your partner.

Talking to your doctor can help

It is important to establish an open relationship with your doctor. Doctors are available to improve and maintain your health, not to make judgments about your sexual decision-making. Doctors can provide you with valuable information about preventing the transmission of STDs, diagnosing an STD, and making sure you get the best possible treatment available should you contract an STD. Talk to your doctor about your sexual practices. Ask questions and address your concerns—that's what doctors are there for!

Being familiar with available health resources is important

A good relationship with someone who can answer your questions or help you find the answers is very helpful.

Try to develop an open relationship with your parents or another trusted adult, such as another relative, teacher, guidance counselor, or boss. While it may seem difficult to talk about sex and health with adults, they may be able to answer your questions or help you find the answers. They will also be able to give you support. Sexual health and STDs can be emotional issues, and having someone to talk to who will listen and offer advice, help, or provide caring is important to your health.

Sexual health is an ongoing process

Maintaining your sexual health is a continual process, not a one-time act. Many people choose to stay healthy by not having sex. If you decide you are not ready to have sex, it is important to remind yourself why you have made that decision and to think of ways to stick to your decision even when it's difficult.

The decision to become sexually active is one that requires the maturity and responsibility to take care of your health and the health of your partners. By talking about protection with sex partners and using condoms each and every time you have sex, you are taking some necessary steps to maintain your sexual health.

Other Concerns about Sex

STDs aren't the only problems we should address when dealing with sex and sexuality. Generally speaking, sex is one activity that should have a positive connotation, yet that's far from the case for many people. If you're experiencing pressure, unease, or apprehension in the context of a sexual situation, perhaps it's a situation to avoid.

Nonetheless, many students continue into a sexual relationship despite multiple warnings, looking for validation, or acceptance in the face of reason. In traveling this route, however, the relationship can have disastrous effects on their self-esteem. When people engage in sexual activity that they don't really want, they tend to feel badly about themselves.

A sexual relationship can also be psychologically harmful when it reflects the pressure to conform to societal norms. Some students feel compelled to relate to those who look or think like them. This suggests it's only "normal" to enter a heterosexual relationship or socialize with members of your race or religion. Thankfully, this belief is growing outdated, and more diverse relationships are slowly gaining acceptance. Understand, though, that starting a relationship to fit others' perceptions will leave you feeling empty if it's not what you truly desire.

Stress and Sex

Seeing the words "stress" and "sex" together might seem odd at first, but both can contribute largely to your concerns and thus harm your overall health. Remember, too, that sex in and of itself can be a powerful stressor in anyone's life. We all recognize that sexuality has a physical aspect, but for many people, it's the psychological impact of sex that proves to be a challenge.

THE EMOTIONAL
What Is Stress?

Imagine that you are a cave-man or -woman. You come out of your cave with the sun up and the birds chirping. You're feeling good. Your heart rate is normal. Suddenly you hear a twig snap, look to your right, and see an enormous saber-toothed tiger! You have two choices. You can either fight the tiger or try to escape it by running. This is called the "fight or flight" reaction to stress. In a life-threatening emergency, the body produces powerful hormones to give you strength to fight or run away. These hormones boost your heart rate and metabolism to give you quick energy. Whether you fight or flee, your stress hormones are consumed and your body returns to normal.

Our problem today is that the stresses we face are not saber-toothed tigers, nor do we do much physical fighting or fleeing. Our stress hormones still accumulate, however, although we no longer use them up.

Is all stress bad? Imagine a world with absolutely none. While the thought is intriguing, the reality would probably bore you with time. Some stress is positive, even essential. For instance, when we run a race, play a game, or act in a play onstage, we experience stress, but it provides excitement and motivation. It's stimulating! When a teacher announces an exam, that stress can cause you to study. Hans Selye, a well-known expert on stress, called this positive type "eustress." He even went so far as to suggest, "Without stress, there could be no life."

Selye describes negative stress as "distress." Distress can have physical symptoms that detract from your good health, including high blood pressure, heart disease, stroke, headaches, stomach pain, and sleeplessness. To interrupt distress before it can do long-term damage, it's helpful to have some effective strategies.

Ways to Manage Stress

- Set your priorities. Tackle your main concerns rather than being pulled in too many directions.
- Exercise. One benefit of exercise is that it significantly reduces stress levels. Even people uninterested in personal fitness find themselves feeling less burnt out when they do exercise.
- Develop relaxation routines. Give yourself time and space to unwind. Create a nurturing environment. For instance, a home free of clutter (e.g., your books, papers, clothes, and dishes are neatly put away) creates a visual sense of order that helps lower your stress levels. To leave a hectic academic world only to return to a chaotic home will only add to your stress.
- Use techniques such as muscle relaxation and visualization to reduce stress.
- Listen to soothing music. Choose music that has a beat that is slower than your heart rate. Classical or New Age music and natural sounds such as water running can be very relaxing.
- Take a few deep breaths. Focus on your breathing. If you concentrate on breathing, it's harder to think about your troubles.

- Lie down in a comfortable place, then tense and relax your muscles. Start with the muscles in your head and work your way down to your toes. Tense each muscle for 5 to 10 seconds, and then release the tension completely.

- Keep your sense of humor. Laughter literally reduces the level of stress hormones.

- Maintain a healthy diet. When we're stressed, we tend to eat too much or too little.

- Use positive thinking. Look for the good things in life and take the time to appreciate them.

- Focus on what you can control. We often waste our precious mental energy on things we can't do anything about.

- Help someone else solve their problem or issue. This may help you put problems in perspective. Helping someone else helps you.

- DO NOT ISOLATE YOURSELF! When you feel most stressed out, that's when to keep in touch. By contemplating your stressors alone, you may be allowing your heightened emotions to produce irrational thoughts and acts.

Problem Solving

Many students find that much of their stress comes from their difficulty with solving the problems that they face. One of the most effective ways of dealing with this sort of stress is to make daily progress. Feelings of helplessness and depression often result from a negative attitude about how we handle problems on a daily basis. Look back to the chapter on Locus of Control and Motivation and realize that you have the power to begin fixing your problems. When you do, your stress will decrease.

The following five steps (the Five D's) lay out a method for dealing with a problem.

1. **Decide** if there is a problem.
2. **Define** the problem.
3. **Develop** a plan for solving your problem.
4. **Do** it.
5. **Double-check** to make sure your problem has been solved.

First, you need to **decide** if there is a problem. The world is not a perfect place, but not everything needs to be "fixed." Some "problems" aren't worth the time and effort it would take to "solve" them. Evaluate your own priorities and desires, and decide what tasks are really worth your time and effort.

Next, you need to **define** the problem in a way that helps you solve it. What is a problem? A problem is really just another name for an unmet goal. For example, if the problem is that you don't have enough money for a new car, this is just another way of saying that your goal is to get a new car. Defining a problem as a goal in this way can help you see that there may be more than one way to achieve it. Look back to the chapter on Goal Setting for more information about how to set achievable goals, and try to define your problems following those guidelines.

Third, **develop** a plan for solving your problem, which is really the same as a plan for achieving your goal. Break the problem down into smaller parts, and figure out which parts to do first. No matter how big the problem, it can always be broken down into smaller steps. The smaller steps themselves can be further broken down into individual tasks. Try to break your plan down into steps that would take no more than 15 to 20 minutes to achieve.

Next, **do** it. Put your plan into action. Avoid procrastination and get started on solving your problems and achieving your goals. Look to the chapter on Time Management for more information on keeping up with your activities and responsibilities.

Finally, **double-check** to make sure that your plan is working. After you have done the first several parts of your plan, you should take time to reevaluate your progress. Are you in fact making progress towards your goal? If so, you can continue to carry out your plans; if not, you may need to develop a new plan.

Once you have succeeded in solving your problem and have achieved your goal, make sure to take time to appreciate your abilities and celebrate your success. This will help reinforce a feeling of power over your situation, and will help you strengthen your internal Locus of Control. This, in turn, will help you feel less stressed-out by your problems.

Psychological Hardiness

We all know people who produce in the face of stress. How do they stay healthy despite high-powered jobs and constant challenge? Psychologists have studied such individuals for their psychological hardiness and ability to deal with stress in a positive way. People who resist stress have a positive attitude toward life and its challenges.

- They are open to change. They view change as a challenge rather than a threat.
- They have a feeling of involvement in whatever they're doing. They are committed to their endeavors.
- They have a sense of control over events rather than a feeling of powerlessness. Having a sense of control is essential to good mental health.

Some of the psychologically hardiest people known to history survived the Nazi concentration camps of World War II. Despite extreme hardship, including witnessing the slaughter of their loved ones, some survived the camps and went on to productive lives. Scientists studying these individuals learned that they employed several resources for survival. Using knowledge and intelligence, for instance, they identified options for dealing with their situations; they could establish a sense of control by choosing the best alternative. These survivors also had a strong sense of identity and were confident, powerful individuals. Researchers also found that a strong social network gave them a collective strength.

RELATIONSHIPS, CONFLICT, AND ANGER

Human beings are a social species. We need relationships. But the ability to form and maintain healthy relationships eludes many. Heck, the divorce rate is more than 50%! Many students have missed out on good role models for marriage. How do two people maintain a relationship that benefits both? It's not easy. Here are a few obstacles to forming and keeping healthy relationships.

Difficulty One: Constant Change

Consider couples A and B. They are just two people, so this should be easy. After all, they've gotten past the hard part: forming a relationship in the first place. Right? Wrong! People change and young people, especially those away from home for the first time, change a great deal. Returning to school as an adult is a major life change as well. In other words, with every passing day, A is taking in and processing new information, which becomes part of A's identity and, in fact, changes A. Here's someone who is changing rapidly, while B is changing just as fast. At that rate, a 50% divorce rate doesn't seem all that bad, does it?

Difficulty Two: Codependency

College students, especially those from out of town, may be desperate to find their niche when they arrive on campus. Many enter an intimate relationship early in their college careers as a result, which can harm their chances of meeting new people and expanding their social networks. It can also lead to a dependency in which the couple's sole happiness lies within the relationship. Generally, this initiates a codependent situation. Codependency is a series of survival techniques employed to maintain the relationship at the individual's expense.

Characteristics of Codependency

- The belief that positive feelings about oneself are derived from one's partner
- An acceptance of blame for everything that goes wrong
- A willingness to spend one's own energies helping others
- The reduction of one's social circle to accommodate the codependent
- The reduction of one's pursuit of personal interests to accommodate the codependent
- A preoccupation with the codependent's emotions at the expense of one's own
- A vacillation in decision-making based on the codependent's opinion
- The tendency to tie one's happiness to the codependent's emotional output
- A new acceptance of previously unacceptable behavior as normal
- The tendency to cover up and lie to protect unacceptable behaviors
- A fear of asking for attention to one's own needs
- The basing of future desires on the codependent's needs or desires

Source: Beattie, Melody (1992) Co-dependent No More: How to Stop Controlling Others and Start Caring for Yourself, Hazelton foundation (42–52).

If some of the above characteristics sound familiar, you may wish to reevaluate whether your relationship is good for you. Remember, we engage in relationships to feel good. They should NOT make us feel depressed or inferior. If you think you may be in this type of relationship, don't try to handle it alone. The chapter on campus resources can help you with finding a mental health counselor and/or authorities who are trained to handle this type of situation.

Difficulty Three: Communication/Conflict Management

Many people just don't know how to ask for what they want. Below are three methods for dealing with conflict:

Passive communication is emotionally dishonest because you're denying your own needs and feelings. The passive communicator frequently allows others to manipulate or take advantage of him- or herself. Not surprisingly, this often results in anger, resentment, or depression. Passive communicators may suffer from chronic ailments—ulcers, headaches, or high blood pressure—since they internalize their conflicts instead of putting them on the table and resolving them. Passive responses have the unconscious effect of absolving one's actions rather than taking responsibility for them.

Aggressive responses are inappropriate and tend to ignore the rights and feelings of others. Those hurt or angered may, in turn, avoid or take revenge against the aggressive communicator. This behavior may get short-term results, but in the long run will damage your relationships. Think about the last time you were verbally attacked. Did it make you care more for that person and want to please him or her? In this chapter, we define aggressive communication as demanding, selfish, hostile, confrontational, or combative. Please note that this form of "aggressiveness" should not be confused with taking the initiative, working energetically, being enterprising, and doing your best.

Assertive communication allows us to express our needs, feelings, opinions, and preferences in a direct and honest manner without threatening, harming, "putting down," or manipulating others. This communication style doesn't guarantee that our needs or wishes will be met, but ensures that we express them in an appropriate manner. In other words, the rights of both parties have been acknowledged and honored.

In striving for a more assertive communication style, we must be mindful that passive and aggressive styles have their uses. Aggression may be an appropriate response to an overzealous sales pitch; passivity may be a good approach to an obnoxious drunk.

Characteristics of a Positive Relationship

By now, you may be saying, "The heck with relationships! They're simply not worth it!" Yes, they seem difficult. Yes, they're hard to maintain. But you can do it. Let's discuss the characteristics of a healthy relationship so as to ease your anxiety.

First, a healthy relationship requires *independence*. Two people can be happy together only when each partner can be happy without the other. As we discussed, in a codependent relationship, the partners don't feel complete or happy when deprived of each other's company or participation. In a healthy relationship, however, one partner can enjoy friends or events without the other while maintaining the same degree of happiness as if the partners were together. Two good examples: separate sets of friends and independent hobbies.

Second, *compromise* in decision making should be a daily endeavor. In fact, couples should compromise on the majority of their joint decisions. Thus, they must learn to give and take. Relationships with dominant and submissive partners are doomed to fail.

Third, healthy relationships require *trust*. Without it, in fact, there can be no relationship. Trust can eliminate the overwhelming majority of problems in a relationship. TRUST IS ESSENTIAL to both interpersonal relationships and personal autonomy. It is based on honesty and respect. Be aware, however, that trust is difficult to build yet can be squandered in an instant.

Finally, in a healthy relationship, lines of *communication* are always open. Needs and concerns are welcomed, not shunned. The partners are free to express their feelings without blame or ridicule.

Dealing with Anger

You *will* get angry. College is rife with experiences that push your buttons. So how do you deal with an old curmudgeon of a professor? A selfish classmate? How you express your anger can determine whether you succeed or fail.

First, acknowledge that you're angry. Many people suppress their anger, hoping it will go away, but this is decidedly incorrect. What may occur, instead, is that suppressed anger will lead to an outburst. You must understand that you have limited space in which to store your emotions. Once you've hit your limit, KA-BOOM! All the emotions you stored up and wouldn't deal with are going to explode. What's more, the flare-up is usually directed at an unintended target at an inopportune time.

Once we recognize our anger, the next step is to find an outlet for it. What will it be? Do we direct our anger at its source, or are we unable to do so straightforwardly and thus must find another form of expression? *Assess the situation before you do anything.* Remember that anger tends to decrease our ability to process information and can even distort certain facts. In other words, elevated levels of emotion can make us irrational.

Having evaluated a situation and decided it's permissible to express anger overtly, how do we do it in a constructive manner? Begin by resisting the temptation to make it a personal

argument. While we might yearn to call the person a knucklehead, the end result will be nothing more than a war of words.

To handle anger overtly, stay on task, name the behavior or action that prompted your reaction, and describe how it's affecting you. When a person is always late to meetings, explain that the group must spend extra time to get the tardy attendee up to speed. Instead of getting personal, stay focused on the behavior and how it affects you. This will make for a much easier conversation.

On the surface, it's easier to express anger covertly than overtly. Covertly, we're simply choosing another outlet, a safer one. This can mean engaging in physical exercise, writing in a journal, or discussing our concerns with a counselor or confidant. That's not to say that there are no destructive means of expressing anger covertly. We could, for instance, allow our anger to be projected onto an unrelated person or object. Let's say you're frustrated at a grade you received on a paper. You are angry at yourself, for lack of effort, and at the instructor who graded you. You'd like to tell the professor what you're thinking, but cannot. So when you arrive home and your dog jumps on you as soon as you walk in the door, you bop him on the nose. This is an expression of suppressed anger that you've built up over your poor grade. Your dog didn't write the paper and he didn't grade it, either. Yet he was punished for it. This is an example of a covert—and unconstructive—expression of anger.

SUMMARY

Students attend college to further their education and boost their chances of entering a meaningful, well-paid profession. Still, the worthiness of your goals shouldn't result in the neglect of your physical, psychological, and social needs. For a healthy and happy life, you must strive to become a well-balanced person, observing with care every aspect of your well-being.

NAME: _____ DATE: _____

WHAT IS YOUR STRESS INDEX?*

Do you frequently: Yes No

 1. Neglect your diet? ☐ ☐
 2. Try to do everything yourself? ☐ ☐
 3. Blow up easily? ☐ ☐
 4. Seek unrealistic goals? ☐ ☐
 5. Fail to see the humor in situations others find funny? ☐ ☐
 6. Act rude? ☐ ☐
 7. Make a big deal out of everything? ☐ ☐
 8. Look to others to make things happen? ☐ ☐
 9. Have difficulty making decisions? ☐ ☐
10. Complain that you're disorganized? ☐ ☐
11. Avoid people whose ideas are different from yours? ☐ ☐
12. Keep everything inside? ☐ ☐
13. Skip exercising? ☐ ☐
14. Have only a few supportive relationships? ☐ ☐
15. Use psychoactive drugs, such as sleeping pills and tranquilizers, without a doctor's approval? ☐ ☐
16. Get too little rest? ☐ ☐
17. Become angry when you're kept waiting? ☐ ☐
18. Ignore symptoms of stress? ☐ ☐
19. Procrastinate? ☐ ☐
20. Believe there is only one right way to do a thing? ☐ ☐
21. Fail to include relaxation in your schedule? ☐ ☐
22. Gossip? ☐ ☐
23. Race through the day? ☐ ☐
24. Spend lots of time lamenting your past? ☐ ☐
25. Fail to take a breather from noise and crowds? ☐ ☐

Score 1 for each yes answer and 0 for each no.

Total score: _____

1–6. There are few hassles in your life. Make sure, though, that you're not trying so hard to avoid problems that you shy away from challenges.

7–13. You've got your life in pretty good control. Work on your choices and habits that cause unnecessary stress.

14–20. You're approaching the danger zone. You may well be suffering stress-related symptoms, and your relationships could be strained. Think carefully about choices you've made. Take breaks to relax.

Above 20. Emergency! You must stop now, rethink how you are living, change your attitudes, and pay scrupulous attention to your diet, exercise, and relaxation programs.

*From Andrew Slaby, Sixty Ways to Make Stress Work for You.

Glossary

Academic advising: advisors help students choose appropriate classes, based on their degree program and career aspirations.

Acronyms: a word formed from the first letter of each major word in a term; an abbreviation (e.g., SMART)

Acrostics: text or poems in which the first letter, syllable, or word of each sentence, paragraph, or other recurring feature spells out another message.

Active Listening: a collaborative activity between student and instructor that requires listening for meaning and understanding then responding with empathy, non-judgment, and asking questions for clarification.

Aggressive response: ignoring the rights and feelings of others; more concerned with protecting own rights and feelings; communication style.

APA (American Psychological Association) style: format used for writing documents in business and psychology courses, as well as in social and natural sciences courses.

Assertive communication: allows to express needs, feelings, opinions, and preferences in a direct and honest manner without threatening, harming, "putting down," or manipulating others; communication style: to understand and to seek a solution.

Association: process of forming mental connections between new pieces of information and something else that you already know.

Attainable goal: goal that is reachable.

Auditory Learning Style: learning that involves listening to an explanation, verbal instructions, lectures, or books on tape.

Basic skills: reading, writing, basic arithmetic, higher level mathematics, listening, and speaking.

Binge drinking: consuming too much alcohol at one time; binge drinkers are at risk for many alcohol-related problems.

Branching diagrams: starts with a main idea and shows how others branch off from it and then from one another.

Budget: itemized list of all your income and expenses.

Career Services Center: located in the Student Union to offer students programs and services to assist them with career planning, career preparation, and career placement.

Charting: study system that allows you to arrange information in a chart format. Helps to compare and contrast multiple topics, events, or people in relation to specific criteria or questions.

Chunking: breaking material into small groups of information to help retain in short term memory.

Codependency: a psychological condition or a relationship in which a person is controlled or manipulated by another who is affected with a pathological condition (as an addiction to alcohol or heroin); *broadly*: dependence on the needs of or control by another.

Compare: bring out points of similarity and points of differences.

Concentration: devoting yourself fully to studying and remembering, not thinking of anything else while doing so.

Concepts or Information Maps: visual guides to topics that may not be sequential by breaking them down from general to specific ideas.

Contrast: show differences when placed side by side.

Cornell Method: a study system method created by Dr. Walter Paulk of Cornell University.

Cover letter: introduces applicant to a prospective employer, explains interest in the company, and highlights most relevant knowledge, skills, abilities, and experiences related to the position.

Credit report: a detailed list of credit history.

Credit score: credit rating based on a set scale of 300–850 points.

Critical thinking: a process of identifying different views, questioning each one, seeking additional information, and then constructing meaning to arrive at a conclusion.

Criticize: give judgment of; approve or disapprove; give good and bad points.

Cultural relativity: the traits of cultures, ethnic groups, genders, and sexual preferences are viewed as different but equally valuable and worthy of respect.

Culture: the behavior, custom, language, and values shared by members of a group. Culture includes all that we learn from the people in our community.

Define: give the meaning of, explain the nature of.

Describe: tell about, give a word picture which characterizes; do not just name a label.

Diagram: make a drawing, chart, plans, or graph, and usually add labels; possibly add a brief explanation.

Discrimination: when people are denied rights or opportunities because of their differences, often due to prejudice and stereotyping.

Discuss: examine or analyze, carefully, and give reasons pro and con. Be complete and give details.

Distress: negative stress resulting in possible mental symptoms or physical symptoms (high blood pressure, heart disease, stroke, headaches, stomach pain, and sleeplessness).

Diverse: the act of differing from one another; being unlike in qualities of elements.

Diversity: the state of being diverse or different.

Eating disorder: an illness, with complex underlying psychological and biological reasons, that cause people to acquire eating habits that are harmful to their bodies.

Enrollment Services: oversees all college records, including transcripts, transient work (temporary transfer) and updating student information.

Enumerate: give a numbered list; name one by one.

Essay question: designed to reveal ability to make and support valid generalizations, or to apply broad principles to specific instances.

Ethical goals: demonstrate the quality of character, an understanding of right from wrong, and the rules that govern us, both professionally and personally.

Ethnicity: refers to a sense of belonging to one particular culture and to sharing its beliefs, experiences, ceremonies, and other traditions. Ethnic groups usually have common ancestors from the same country or geographic area.

Eustress: positive or healthy stress that helps us perform, and results in a favorable outcome.

Evaluate: carefully appraise the problem, citing both advantages and limitations; emphasize the appraisal of experts and, to a lesser degree, your own evaluation.

Evaluative situations: being observed or evaluated by others.

Exam: refers to the midterm and final examinations; each can cover several tests' worth of material.

Exercise: a form of physical activity that is performed or practiced to improve physical fitness.

Expenses: those things that are paid for on an ongoing basis such as rent and utilities.

Explain: cite both advantages and disadvantages; include appraisal of authorities and your own appraisal.

External Distractions: something outside the body that causes a reaction and thus can affect concentration. Examples are people talking, music, TV or cell phones ringing.

External Locus of Control: a belief that factors outside of yourself, luck, or others control what happens to you, your success, or failures.

Extrinsic Motivation: inspired to learn for external reasons, such as pleasing family, friends, a teacher, or employer.

FACTS.org: (Florida Academic Counseling and Tracking for Students). This service provides free online advising and is a place for students to plan and track their academic progress beginning in middle school and continuing through college.

Fight or flight response: the mind and body becomes alert to an attack or the need to escape from a threat.

Financial Aid Office: helps students determine their eligibility for financial aid at TCC.

Fixed expenses: the same every month such as rent, car loan, phone, insurance and gas.

Flexible expenses: vary depending on behavior such as entertainment, fast food, and new clothes.

Follow up or thank you letter: short note written after an interview to thank the interviewer for taking the time to talk. Email, handwritten note or a typed letter.

Food guide pyramid: a food pyramid is a pictorial representation of a diet that makes recommendations of how much a person should consume from each food group every day.

Gender, Sex: "gender" refers to the ways we distinguish males from females, since different cultures raise men and women to act in specific ways. Refer to sex.

Goals: objectives that should be specific, measureable, attainable, realistic, and timely.

GPA: grade point average

Illustrate: make clear by showing an example.

Income: earnings from working each month or from other sources, such as a student loan.

Informal Indent Outline: a note-taking system that requires the recording of main ideas and concepts on the left with major and minor details underneath in a bulleted fashion and descending order.

I-Notes: a note-taking system developed by Daniel Walther that requires the use of a large "I" drawn in the center of a page, and the recording of main ideas on the left, details on the right, and questions at the bottom of the page.

Instructor-generated tests: drawn from the instructor's own question bank; typically, these test questions come from material presented in class.

Internal Distractions: internal things that can affect your concentration, such as hunger or muscle aches, depression, anxiety, and fatigue.

Internal Locus of Control: belief that you have control over your success and failures, and they are a direct reflection of your actions.

Interpret: translate, give examples, and usually give your judgment.

Intrinsic Motivation: being motivated to do something by internal factors, because it brings you personal pleasure or for the common good. The motivation comes from within a person.

Justify: prove a point, give an argument; discuss bad and good points and conclude with its good reasons.

Learning Commons: one-stop source for learning assistance in with math, science, business related, reading, writing, and language courses. Additionally, students can find diagnostic assessments, electronic resources, tutoring, technology and multi-media support, computers, and more.

Learning Style: preferred way of acquiring new information.

List: a simple series of words or numerals (as the names of persons or objects), official roster

Locus of Control: personal belief regarding what controls behavior: the factors and personal experience that cause success or failure in meeting goals. Refer to Personal responsibility.

Long-term goals: what you plan to achieve in the next few years.

Long-term memory: information that is stored and accessed for use at a later time.

Major: an area of study to pursue while in college and results in a degree.

Measureable goal: establishes concrete criteria for measuring progress toward the attainment of a goal; can be answered by asking how much, how many, how will I know when it is accomplished.

Memorization Techniques: techniques to learn and retain information.

Memory: the brain's ability to store and access information that has been acquired through life experiences.

Mental block: to freeze up and forget everything that has been studied.

MLA (Modern Languages Association) style: the most widely used style format in general education courses and is preferred in most English and humanities courses.

Mnemonics: the use of tricks, games, or rhymes to help you remember.

Motivation: inspiration and commitment to achieve a goal, whether academic, professional, or personal.

Multiple intelligences: how people learn and what makes them successful in school and in life.

My Success Plan: an academic plan developed by students which includes a major and the university prerequisites.

Negative Cash Flow: expenses are more than income.

Note taking strategies/system: provides a useful, convenient record for study and review.

Nutrition: the act or process of nourishing or being nourished; *specifically:* the sum of the processes by which an animal or plant takes in and utilizes food substances.

Objective questions: have one specific answer, with little variation in the acceptable response.

On campus courses: face to face courses. They may also use some instruction on the web.

Outline: give the main ideas in organized arrangement; use heading and subheadings to give a well-ordered list.

Passive communication: denying needs and feelings; failing to express how we honestly feel.

Performance anxiety: a feeling one might have in a situation that carries great pressure to succeed.

Personal goals: goals that should be driven and identified by your values, beliefs, passions, and dreams.

Personal qualities: responsibility, self-esteem, sociability, self-discipline, and integrity.

Personal responsibility: protecting and nurturing your health and emotional well-being by communicating your needs assertively in your relationships is a part of taking self-responsibility for your actions.

Plagiarism: present an idea or product, derived from an existing source, as a new and original one.

Positive Cash Flow: expenses are less than income.

Prejudice: a prior, often incomplete judgment of a person, group or idea.

Prioritize: decide what is most important and do that first.

Problem solving: the cognitive or thought processes used to solve a difficult situation or problem.

Process diagrams: shows the methods, steps, and stages that describe how events occur.

Procrastination: habitually delaying or postponing activities.

Prove: establish that something is true by citing facts or giving logical reasons.

Publisher-generated test: drawn from a test bank supplied by the textbook publisher; the questions on these tests focus mostly on material from the book.

Quiz: covers a class to a week's worth of material, depending on the instructor.

Race: refers to groups seen as different due to physical traits such as facial features and the color of their eyes, skin, and hair.

Racism: when one race or ethnic group holds a negative attitude or perception of another. It is prejudice based on race.

Realistic goal: represents an objective towards which you are both willing and able to work.

Relate: stress association or connections between ideas.

Repetition: the act of stating again or saying over from memory.

Resumé: summarizes your qualifications, skills, education, and work experience; no longer than one or two pages.

Review: analyze a subject critically.

Rhyming: a simple rhyming phrase or song can help you remember something that may be difficult to memorize.

Screening interview: matches the capabilities of potential employees with the needs of the company.

Selection interview: enables an interviewee to meet with the decision maker or a committee, so that they can determine the interviewee's qualifications, as well as see how well the interviewee interacts with other members of the team.

Self-knowledge: understanding yourself and taking pride in your unique qualities, values, personality, interests, and talents.

Self-paced courses: independent study courses in which students work at their own pace over the 16 weeks required to complete each course.

Sensory memory: deals with information received through your five senses: sight, hearing, touch, smell, and taste; discarded from memory after a few seconds.

Sex: refers to anatomical differences. Refer to Gender.

Sexism: a negative attitude or perception based on sex or gender.

Sexually Transmitted Disease: an illness, infection, disease, that is spread through sexual intercourse or sexual contact.

Short-term goals: measured easily and accomplished in a relatively short time; an hour, a day, a week, or a semester.

Short-term memory: includes all the information currently being processed in a person's brain and it's generally thought to have a very limited capacity; lasts 30–60 seconds.

SMART: an acronym used for setting good goals; goals should be specific, measureable, attainable, realistic, and timely.

Specific goal: a goal that is detailed and definite; can be answered by applying the six W questions: who, what, when, where, which, why.

SQ3R method: a study system used to help students improve their reading and studying of textbooks, articles, reports, etc.

State: presents the main points briefly.

Stereotype: a generalization that expresses conventional or biased ideas about people in a certain group.

Stress: body's (emotional or physical) response to pressures or demands in our environment.

Student Access Card: an ID card for using TCC services such as the library, Lifetime Sports Complex, and student computer labs. The card also allows free rides on the Tallahassee Star Metro buses, free or reduced access to county parks and recreation, and more.

Student Success Center: houses counselors to assist students with counseling on a variety of levels such as academic advising, career planning, transfer and scholarship information, and assistance with questions of a more personal nature.

Study condition: desk or table with adequate writing area, plenty of space for books and a sturdy, comfortable chair.

Study environment: one place that is comfortable for studying and that is used consistently.

Study location: a designated study area.

Study ratio: represents the number of hours of study per hour of class.

Subjective questions: have several correct responses such as, short answer and essay questions.

Summarize: give the main points briefly.

Tactile Learning Style: prefers learning that involves hands-on activities, interactive games, and tutorials. Also referred to as kinesthetic learning style.

Tangible goal: experience the goal with one of your senses.

TCC Passport: the student portal that provides students' access to Blackboard, their TCC student email account and other online resources by logging in once.

Televised courses: delivered over a local television station at any given time.

Test Anxiety: overwhelming feelings of nervousness and lack of control one might experience resulting in difficulties taking a test or demonstrating knowledge on a test.

Test: covers a chapter to several weeks' worth of material.

Thinking skills: creative thinking, decision making, problem solving, mental visualization, knowing how to learn, and reasoning.

Time management: the effective use of time through skills, techniques, and tools for accomplishing our long term and short term goals, as well as our daily tasks and activities.

Timeline: schedule of events within a specific period with a planned order of occurrence.

Timely goal: a goal that is grounded within a timeframe.

Trace: give a description of progress in a definite order; follow the trail.

Turabian or Chicago style: a style format used in history and religion courses.

Value system: the sum total of all one's values; the basis for goals.

Values: standards for shaping who we are and who we desire to be; they are standards for personal and professional behavior.

Visual Learning Style: learning that involves reading, demonstrations, videos, images, flash cards, and diagram.

Visualize: to make a mental picture of what to remember.

Web based courses: courses delivered via the Internet.

Work ethic: reflects the importance attached to what one does for a living.

Workplace competencies: the knowledge, skills, abilities, and personal qualities that are required to succeed on a job.